THE
Malt File

The
MALT WHISKY
Association

THE Malt File

The Malt Whisky Association's guide to single malt whiskies and their distilleries

Tasting notes by
John Lamond

Background and history by
Robin Tuček

Published by The Edinburgh Publishing Company Limited,
Admiral House,
30 Maritime Street,
Leith, Edinburgh EH6 6SE

©The Master of Malt Limited 1989, 1991 and 1993

First edition published by Benedict Books on behalf of
The Malt Whisky Association June 1989
Reprinted 1991
Second edition published 1993

British Library Cataloguing-in-Publication Data.
A catalogue record for this book is available from the British Library.

ISBN 1 874201 15 3

Cover photograph courtesy of Bushmills Limited

Printed and bound in the United Kingdom by BPCC Wheatons Ltd

Contents

Introduction

Scotch Whisky has within it a distillation of the colours, flavours and atmosphere of Scotland. Scotland's soft air, water, agriculture and traditional craftsmanship combine to produce the world's premier spirit. This second edition of The Malt File is a homage to the world craftsmen of the industry.

I was weaned on Scotch Whisky (sorry, Mum) and, although I had drunk malt whiskies in my youth, the bulk of this youthful consumption was blended. I didn't really discover the magic of malt until 1975, when Dewar's, for whom I was working at the time, introduced "Dewar's Pure Malt", a vatted malt. My curiosity was aroused.

I visited Aberfeldy distillery, which was operated by SMD and for which Dewar's held the licence, was taken round by Ricky Robertson, who was the manager at the time, and with him I tasted cask samples of three vintages. I was hooked.

When The Malt Whisky Association asked me to put the tasting notes together for a publication which they had in mind, I was first of all flattered - until the enormity of my task dawned upon me. I discovered early on that, in order to remain objective, I could sample a maximum of three whiskies at any one time and only at certain times of the day. Thus I have had to be very clinical in my tasting practices - which has made the chore a little unattractive for those who have offered to assist me in my endeavours.

I am frequently asked by these people, "What is your favourite malt?". Taste is a very personal thing and my choice isn't necessarily yours. In any case, I do not have any one favourite. I enjoy a lighter malt around lunchtime, or earlier in the day, something with more body around 5 or 6 p.m., one of the heavier malts at night, and at 3 a.m. in the morning....!

I have learnt a great deal since the publication of the first edition in 1989 and some of this knowledge is incorporated in this second edition. I hope you can also benefit from this knowledge.

Slainte,

John Lamond
Master of Malt

You take the Highland...

No two single malt whiskies are alike. Even malts produced by sister distilleries using the same source of water have their own distinct individuality. But, although single malt whiskies cannot be neatly packaged and parcelled, certain whiskies do have shared characteristics which, although broadly defined, can help to identify a malt's original provenance. For example, some, but not all, Island malts share similarities, as do some Speyside whiskies, particularly those in that elastic glen, Glenlivet.

Traditional Regions

The traditional regions are Highland, Lowland, Islay and Campbeltown, although the latter's once numerous distilleries have now dwindled to just two. It is possible also to sub-divide the Highland region into Speyside, Northern Highland, Eastern Highland, Perthshire and Island (not to be confused with Islay) malts.

Islay Malts

Islay malts are the weightiest, most pungent and most heavily peated and are therefore generally the easiest to identify. These malts take their characteristics both from the peat used to dry the barley and their closeness to the sea. These factors give them what is often described as a seaweedy, medicinal taste and a distinct peaty flavour.

Lowland Malts

Lowland malts are drier when compared to their Highland counterparts and, although often quite spirity, are light whiskies which generally have fewer individual differences than the whiskies from other regions.

Northern Highland Malts

Northern Highland malts are sweeter and have more body and character than their Lowland relations. They can have very distinctive and subtle characters, with a rich mellowness and fullness of flavour, but, equally, they can show a dry peatiness or a delicate fragrance.

Speyside Malts

The Speyside malts are the sweetest whiskies. Although they do

You take the Highland...

not have as much body as other Highland malts, their flavours are richer and more complex with fruity, leafy and honeyed notes and a subtle delicacy of aroma which, once recognised, should be easy to identify.

Eastern Highland Malts
Eastern Highland malts come from the area between Aberdeen and Speyside. Often full- bodied, they tend to have a dry, fruity-sweet flavour, together with a touch of smokiness.

Perthshire Malts
The Perthshire malts, although Highland by definition, come from the area bordering the Lowland region. They tend to be medium-sweet, clean tasting whiskies which are both light and fruity. Their identity may be best considered as falling somewhere between that of Lowland and Speyside whiskies.

The Island Malts
The Island malts from Skye, Jura, Mull and Orkney are characterised by a peaty, smoky nose and flavour. Some could be said to more closely resemble Islay malts while others are more like Northern Highland whiskies.

Campbeltown
If it is possible to categorise Campbeltown nowadays, then it must fall between the Lowlands and the Highlands in dryness, but shows a distinct smoky character with good body.

Irish Malt Whiskey
Irish malt whiskey is much lighter, smoother and fresher than its Scottish counterpart. This is, in part, due to the fact that it is triple distilled, although there are two or three Scottish single malts also produced in this way.

Although it is possible to map out generalised characteristics for single malts, each distillery produces a malt which has its own unique personality. It has its own micro-climate, wild yeasts, source of water and specified malting requirements. All of these factors (and even the shape of the still used) will have an effect on the individual character and flavour of a malt.

Scotland's Malt Distilleries
The Speyside Malts

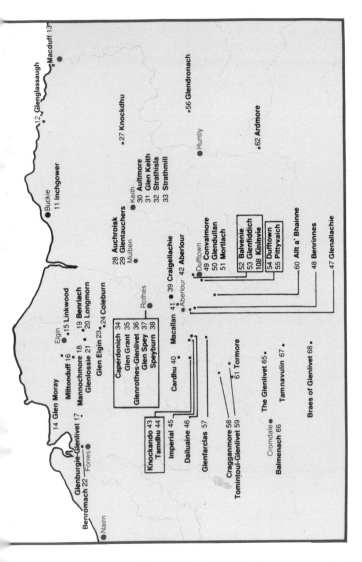

© Bartholomew. Extract from WHISKY MAP OF SCOTLAND.
Reproduced by kind permission.

Scotland's Malt Distilleries

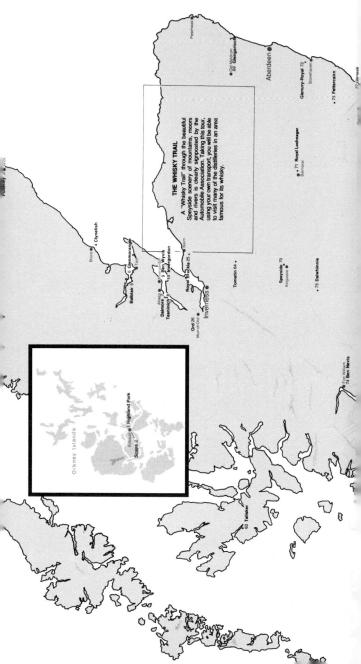

THE WHISKY TRAIL

A "Whisky Trail" through the beautiful Speyside scenery of mountains, moors and rivers is clearly signposted by the Automobile Association. Taking this tour, using your own transport, you will be able to visit many of the distilleries in an area famous for its whisky.

Peterhead

• Old Meldrum
69 **Glengarioch**

Aberdeen •

Glenury-Royal 72

Stonehaven •

• 75 **Fettercairn**

77 Montrose

• 71 **Royal Lochnagar**
Balmoral

Tomatin 64 •

Speyside 70 •
Kingussie

• 73 **Dalwhinnie**

4 Clynelish

Brora •

6 **Glenmorangie**
Tain •

Balblair 5 •

9 **Ben Wyvis**
Alness •

Dalmore •
Teaninich 8 • 10 **Invergordon**

Royal Brackla 25 •
Nairn •

Ord 26 •
Muir of Ord •

Inverness •

Pulteney 3 •

Fort William •
74 **Ben Nevis**

Orkney Islands

• **Highland Park**
Kirkwall •
Scapa 2

63 **Talisker**

The Art of "Nosing"

It seems somewhat perverse that those who most appreciate the finest spirit in the world spend a great deal of their time not drinking it. They do not even go so far as serious-minded wine connoisseurs who swill it round their mouths before ejecting it. No, the master blender will use nothing other than his nose - and his experience - to assess and evaluate malt whisky. The reason for this is to preserve the ability to "taste" after the first sample. The reasoning behind this is simple: unlike wine or other less alcoholic substances, a distilled spirit will anaesthetise the taste buds, the very taste mechanisms which need to be used time and time again.

Aromatics

Our sense of aromatics (or "volatiles" as they are sometimes called) is derived from an organ known as the olfactory epithelium, which is directly linked to the brain. This is located at the back of the nasal passage and is one of the main reasons why we cannot taste so well when we have a cold.

Using the nose to detect aromatic ingredients provides a more immediate route to this area than via the back of the throat. The palate can only detect four taste elements: salt, sweet, sour and bitter. All other flavour characters are created when the palate warms the contents of your mouth and causes aromas to rise through your nasal passages to the olfactory epithelium. There is, of course, a slight difference in the result and the strength of individual flavours may vary, but, in general, the palate should merely confirm the aromas detected by the nose.

Our sense of smell is one of the most under-used of the human senses, being relegated in most cases by sight and taste to a subordinate role and only called into use for rather crude analysis of whether something smells "good" or "bad". In fact, it is one of the most subtle of the senses, capable of detecting even faint changes in style or balance, and having a large "vocabulary" of its own. The tasting vocabulary used throughout this book has evolved over the years and, we hope, is easily comprehended by the reader.

The Master Blender

A master blender has an "educated" nose and can detect more than 150 separate flavours or characters in a whisky.

The Art of "Nosing"

Some of these will tell him that the product has been adversely affected in some way during maturation; others will indicate the type or style of wood in which it has matured. But although you, the malt whisky drinker, do not have senses as highly tuned as the blender, each whisky has a sufficient number of different characteristics to enable you to distinguish one from another.

The Nosing

In general, the nosing of malt whiskies is carried out in a small, tulip shaped or similar glass which, being bulbous at the base and reducing to a relatively narrow rim, releases the aromatics and concentrates them at the rim, where the nose can pick up aromas. The sample is always diluted, or cut, with water; this releases the esters and aldehydes and thus makes the aroma bigger, the amount of water to be added depending on the alcoholic strength of the spirit which is being nosed. As a rough guide, malt whisky in the strength band 40 - 43% alcohol by volume (abv) should be cut with one third water, preferably a soft water - Scottish spring water - or clean tap water. Avoid any water with a high mineral or chlorine content, as these will impart that flavour to the sample.

Higher Strength Whiskies

Other, higher strength whiskies should be cut with a greater quantity of water to reduce the sample to approximately the same strength. A high strength whisky of, for example 60% abv, should be diluted with twice its volume of water for sampling. There is a very good reason for this. The olfactory senses are adversely affected by the higher alcoholic content, even to the extent of feeling pain. Dilution removes the likelihood of this pain being inflicted. The quantity used for sampling should be fairly small, to allow plenty of room for the aromatics to collect in the glass. There is quite enough spirit for an adequate assessment in a diluted single measure of 25ml of whisky and water.

You will find that different elements in the sample become dominant at different periods of the nosing. You may confuse yourself by concentrating too hard with, very often, your first opinion being the correct one. As you become more expert, you will discover a greater range of aromas in the glass. For example, one person may detect rubber in a whisky, while that same characteristic may come over to another as something else - liquorice, for example. The difficulty with either tasting or nosing is in the descriptions used by individuals to describe sensation or flavour. Some attempt has been made to categorise these and John Lamond produced a Malt Whisky Wheel for Aberlour Distillery in an attempt to help identify these characteristics.

While a standardised approach is sensible in that a common language can be created, the sense of smell is very subjective. Malt whisky is a gregarious spirit, so that the next time you are with friends discussing flavour, let your nose lead your opinions. You can still have as much fun trying to describe the aromas in your own words as you will get from finally drinking the whiskies. This is the fascination of single malts. From the same basic simple ingredients comes an enormous variety of styles and tastes which you are now beginning to explore!

A Note on the Water

Although water from a kitchen tap is safe to drink in many parts of the world, it is far from ideal as an accompaniment to malt whisky. In some areas, the water is naturally quite chalky or has a high mineral content. In others, for reasons of public health, various additives are put into water supplies. In Britain, for example, varying amounts of chlorine are added to drinking water. Such chemically treated water is not ideal if you wish to experience the true flavours and aromas of your single malt.

Water filters can be an answer, but even they cannot refresh the water. In a perfect world, the water which we would add would come from the distillery's own water supply.... As an alternative, clear, pure spring water with a low mineral content, such as one of the bottled Scottish waters, which are soft, is eminently suitable.

Choose a still water rather than a sparkling one and avoid the more strongly flavoured waters. They may be excellent as a drink in their own right, but they adversely affect the delightful aromas of malt whiskies. Finally, don't be put off adding water. The belief that nothing but more malt whisky should be added to malt whisky is a misconception. Try it for yourself; one glass with one third water and one without. Your enjoyment will be enhanced.

File Notes

The notes in this book have been compiled in alphabetical order of available brands of whisky, not by distillery or bottler. Where the whisky is from an independent source, this has been noted in the tasting notes.

Single Malts

Remember that most of the malts covered in this book are single malts - the product of one named distillery only. If the term "single malt" is to be used on the label, then the blending of these whiskies may only be carried out with other malts from the same distillery.

Vatted Malts

"Vatted malts" are whiskies from more than one malt distillery which have been blended together according to the specifications of the blender, to produce a fine, consistent product. This may well be given an individual name (such as *Poit Dhubh*). Some vatted malts have been included in a section at the end of the book - as have some single malts bottled under "brand names" other than that of the distillery.

Certain companies are mentioned throughout the text, in abbreviated form. The principal ones are:

IDV   International Distillers and Vintners
DCL   The Distillers Company Limited, now United Distillers (U.D.) a part of Guinness plc
SMD   Scottish Malt Distillers - the malt distilling operational arm of DCL.
IDG   Irish Distillers Group

The Independent Bottlers

Gordon and MacPhail

Based in Elgin, Moray, possibly the foremost independent and partially responsible for the availability of so many bottled single malts
Tel: 0343 545111

Wm. Cadenhead

Based in Campbeltown and owned by J. & A. Mitchell of Springbank, the company also has a shop in Edinburgh's Royal Mile
Tel: 031 556 5864

File Notes

The Vintage Malt Company

A young company, based in Bearsden, Glasgow and specialising in single cask bottlings, as well as one vatted and two single malts under their own brand names Tel: 041 942 4750

Signatory

Based in Leith, Edinburgh, this company offers a wide selection of whiskies. The company also bottles The Master of Malt whiskies Tel: Signatory 031 555 4988. Tel: The Master of Malt 0892 513295

The Malt File is intended as a guide to help you, the consumer, find your way around the different flavours of malt whisky. The historical and geographical notes have been included to heighten your awareness of the distillery locations and environments.

The Master of Malt Rating System

In this, the second edition, we have included our own exclusive *Master of Malt* rating system for *Sweetness*, *Peatiness* and *Availability*. This system is *not* a qualitative system. All malt whiskies are made to similar quality levels, but all have different tastes. Only *YOU* can decide which whiskies are your favourite. The scales run from ❶ to ❿ with ❶ being the driest and least peated, ❿ the sweetest and most pungent. The ratings are a statement of fact; a guide to help you find a malt whisky which is akin to your taste. If, for example, you like a malt with a *Sweetness* factor of ❼ and a *Peatiness* factor of ❹, then those other malts which have a similar rating should suit your palate.

Obviously the bottlings from the independents are necessarily finite. We have given their bottlings an *Availability* rating of ❹; if the vintage listed is completely depleted, then they normally follow up with the next vintage which should, making allowances for individual cask influences, be very similar to its predecessor. The *Availability* factors ❶ - ❸ mean that these whiskies are difficult to obtain; ❹ - ❻ are available from the specialist merchants; ❼ - ❿ are increasingly more widely available.

Distillery No.
Refers to position on WHISKY MAP OF SCOTLAND.

File Notes

Vocabulary

We feel that, as any tasting note is necessarily a very personal and subjective thing, some of the descriptions may need some explanation, in particular for readers outwith Scotland. *Tablet* is a Scottish confection, similar to a firm fudge, very sweet and sugary. We have "created" some words which pedants might object to - for this we apologise. Some of these are: *toffeeyed* meaning having the character of toffee; *cerealy*, having the aromas of the grain from which the malt is produced; *mashy*, retaining the aromas from the mash tun. We hope that our manipulation of the language does not upset too many of you and that our reasons for this are understood!

Labels

In some cases, the labels depicted above the tasting notes are not the vintage tasted. This is usually because of the bottler "following" on with the next vintage - which has not yet been tasted. The current vintage should be very similar to the previous vintage when the whisky is bottled at a similar age. It is only where there are older, or younger, ages that these slight nuances become very noticeable differences.

Visitors

 indicates that the distillery welcomes visitors.

Key to Symbols

The following symbols are used at the head of each entry to denote the geographical area of production. For a comparison, see the article on pages 5 and 6.

H Highland

L Lowland

I Islay

S Speyside

C Campbeltown

IR Irish

Hints on Pronunciation...

Unless you are an expert Gaelic speaker, you may have difficulty in pronouncing some of the names of the malts in this book or the areas in which they are produced. The following list contains those that may cause a slight problem, with their phonetic alternatives in italics, thus:

Aberlour	*Aber-lower*
Allt-a' Bhainne	*Olt-a-vane*
Auchentoshan	*Ochentoshen*
Auchroisk	*Othrusk*
Balmenach	*Bal-MAY-nach*
Bruichladdich	*Brew-ich-laddie*
Bunnahabhain	*Boon-a-havun*
Caol Ila	*Kaal-eela*
Cardhu	*Kar-doo*
Clynelish	*Klyn-leesh*
Craigellachie	*Krai-GELLachy*
Dailuaine	*Dall-YEWan*
Dallas Dhu	*Dallas Doo*
Edradour	*Edra-dower*
Glen Garioch	*Glen Gee-ree*
Glenglassaugh	*Glen Glass-och*
Glen Mhor	*Glen Voar*
Glenmorangie	*Glen-MORanjee*
Glentauchers	*Glen-tockers*
Glenury-Royal	*Glen-you-ree*
Islay	*Eye-la*
Knockdhu	*Nock-doo*
Laphroaig	*La-froyg*
Old Pulteney	*Pult-nay*
Pittyvaich	*Pit-ee-vay-ich*
St. Magdalene	*Magdaleen*
Strathisla	*Strath-eye-la*
Tamdhu	*Tam-DOO*
Tamnavulin	*Tamna-VOO-lin*
Teaninich	*Tee-an-inich*
Tomintoul	*Tomin-towel*
Tullibardine	*Tully Bard-eye-n*
and finally...	
Slainte (Cheers!)	*Schlan-jer*

Aberfeldy **H**

Distillery	Aberfeldy
Established	1896
Address	Aberfeldy, Perthshire
Map Ref.	NN 866495
Distillery No.	82

The MASTER of Malt

ABERFELDY

13 years old

SINGLE HIGHLAND MALT WHISKY
Distilled 15th December 1992
Bottled November 1992
A limited edition bottling from cask no. 7789

Established in 1896, this Perthshire distillery is licenced to John Dewar & Sons Ltd. Aberfeldy is the last of several distilleries that once existed in the area. Its water source is the Pitilie Burn.

70cl   Produce of Scotland   43% vol

Bottled exclusively in Scotland for The Master of Malt

History | Built between 1896-8 by Perth-based blenders, John Dewar & Sons Ltd. Owned by Scottish Malt Distillers since 1930, having passed into the ownership of DCL in 1925. Now part of United Distillers plc.

Geography | Immediately to the east of the village on the main (now closed) railway line, main road and close to the river Tay.

Notes | Major rebuilding work took place in 1972, with four stills in a new stillhouse. Previously about a dozen distilleries had been opened in the Aberfeldy neighbourhood by men who had been smugglers in the mountains in earlier times.

Water | Pitilie Burn.

Age/Strength | *13 YEARS 43% abv*

Tasting Notes

Degree of: | Sweetness: ❺ Peatiness: ❼ Availability: ❷
Colour | Very pale straw with lemon tinges
Nose | Fresh, medium-bodied with fruity character and an earthy smokiness
Flavour | Fresh, medium-dry and smooth with an orangey fruitiness
Finish | Quite long, fresh and rich
Notes | Master of Malt bottling, cask no. 7786-7

Age/Strength | *15 YEARS 43% abv*

Tasting Notes

Degree of: | Sweetness: ❼ Peatiness: ❼ Availability: ❹
Colour | Straw/amber with gold highlights
Nose | Quite full and ripe with rich oaky vanilla, creamy, lanolin oiliness with a slight nuttiness
Flavour | Full, smooth, round and medium-sweet with layers of oak at the back
Finish | Full, round and rich, smooth and almost luscious
Notes | United Distillers bottling

Age/Strength Tasting Notes	*1970 DISTILLATION 40% abv*
Degree of:	Sweetness: ❻ Peatiness: ❼ Availability: ❹
Colour	Straw/golden with yellow highlights
Nose	Fresh, crisp, slightly peaty, surprisingly so for a malt so far south
Flavour	Big, round, dry, slightly woody and malty
Finish	Reasonably long and clear
Notes	Gordon & MacPhail bottling

Age/Strength Tasting Notes	*1974 DISTILLATION 40% abv*
Degree of:	Sweetness: ❻ Peatiness: ❼ Availability: ❹
Colour	Straw/amber, gold highlights with a hint of green
Nose	Quite full, earthy, medium-sweet, quite peaty for the region, with hints of hazelnuts
Flavour	Medium-dry, quite full and rich with a slightly oily smoothness
Finish	Rich, slightly spicy with a touch of bitter chocolate and a smokiness on the tail
Notes	Gordon & MacPhail bottling

ABERFELDY DISTILLERY

Aberlour   S

Distillery	Aberlour
Established	1826
Address	Aberlour, Banffshire
Map Ref.	NJ 264424
Distillery No.	42

History — Founded in 1826 by James Gordon and Peter Weir. Rebuilt in 1879 after a fire. Re-equipped with four stills in 1973. This is the date which appears on the label. The Aberlour Glenlivet Distillery Company is a subsidiary of Campbell Distillers, itself part of Pernod Ricard.

Geography — Aberlour is situated about a quarter of a mile below the Lynn of Ruthrie, a 30 foot cascade on Ben Rinnes which falls into the pool which gives rise to the Burn called the Lour. The distillery is about 300 yards from the Lour's confluence with the River Spey.

Notes — Aberlour is a delightful village by the Lour at the foot of Ben Rinnes, from the summit of which ten counties, from Caithness to Perth, are visible. The early Christian missionary, St. Dunstan (or St. Droston, as he was known in Scotland) used the waters of the Lour for baptisms.

Water — A spring on Ben Rinnes.

Age/Strength — *5 YEARS 40% abv*

Tasting Notes

Degree of: Sweetness: ❼ Peatiness: ❹ Availability: ❺
Colour — Very pale, yellowy green with pale yellow highlights
Nose — Green fruit with a hint of sweetness, slightly mashy and a green hedgerow aroma
Flavour — Lightish, spirity, quite round and nutty with a touch of sweetness
Finish — Spicy, almondy and quite good length
Notes — Campbell Distillers bottling purchased in Italy

Age/Strength — *10 YEARS 40% abv*

Tasting Notes

Degree of: Sweetness: ❼ Peatiness: ❺ Availability: ❷
Colour — Deep amber/golden
Nose — Full, rich, sweet, slightly toffee-like
Flavour — Fine, well balanced richness
Finish — Good, full and long

Age/Strength	*1970 DISTILLATION 19 YEARS 43% abv*
Tasting Notes	
Degree of:	Sweetness: ❼ Peatiness: ❺ Availability: ❷
Colour	Pale to mid-amber with yellow/gold highlights
Nose	Quite full-bodied, medium-sweet, rich, soft and almost honeyed with a slight oily note
Flavour	Full, medium-sweet, a touch of sherry-nuttiness, smooth and spicy
Finish	Rich, nutty, fresh and delicately smoky
Notes	Master of Malt bottling - cask nos. 236-9

Age/Strength	*1970 DISTILLATION 21 YEARS 43% abv*
Tasting Notes	
Degree of:	Sweetness: ❼ Peatiness: ❹ Availability: ❺
Colour	Deep, bright amber with rich old gold highlights
Nose	Quite fresh, lanolin oily character, ripe, almost walnut character with a touch of hedgerow greenness at the back
Flavour	Medium-dry, full, fresh, walnuts, creamily smooth with a touch of spice and hint of citrus
Finish	Long, clean, creamy with gentle smokiness on the tail
Notes	Campbell Distillers bottling

ABERLOUR-GLENLIVET DISTILLER

20

Allt-a' Bhainne S

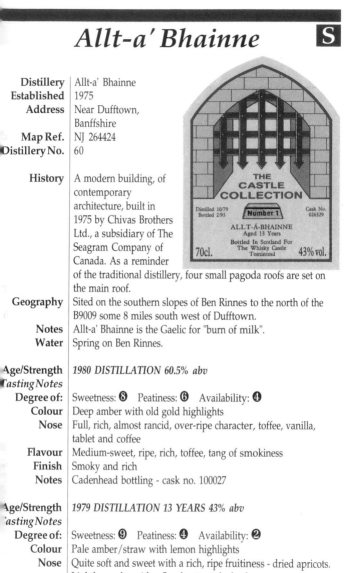

Distillery	Allt-a' Bhainne
Established	1975
Address	Near Dufftown, Banffshire
Map Ref.	NJ 264424
Distillery No.	60

History | A modern building, of contemporary architecture, built in 1975 by Chivas Brothers Ltd., a subsidiary of The Seagram Company of Canada. As a reminder of the traditional distillery, four small pagoda roofs are set on the main roof.

Geography | Sited on the southern slopes of Ben Rinnes to the north of the B9009 some 8 miles south west of Dufftown.

Notes | Allt-a' Bhainne is the Gaelic for "burn of milk".

Water | Spring on Ben Rinnes.

Age/Strength | *1980 DISTILLATION 60.5% abv*
Tasting Notes

Degree of: | Sweetness: ❽   Peatiness: ❻   Availability: ❹
Colour | Deep amber with old gold highlights
Nose | Full, rich, almost rancid, over-ripe character, toffee, vanilla, tablet and coffee
Flavour | Medium-sweet, ripe, rich, toffee, tang of smokiness
Finish | Smoky and rich
Notes | Cadenhead bottling - cask no. 100027

Age/Strength | *1979 DISTILLATION 13 YEARS 43% abv*
Tasting Notes

Degree of: | Sweetness: ❾   Peatiness: ❹   Availability: ❷
Colour | Pale amber/straw with lemon highlights
Nose | Quite soft and sweet with a rich, ripe fruitiness - dried apricots. Lightly smoky with a floral note at the back
Flavour | Soft, quite sweet, smooth and round with a fruity character and gently peated.
Finish | Long, smooth soft and almost stickily sweet
Notes | Cask no. 026329, distilled 10/79 and bottled 2/93 for The Whisky Castle of Tomintoul

An Cnoc

Distillery	Knockdhu
Established	1893/4
Address	Knock, Banffshire
Map Ref.	NJ 547528
Distillery No.	27

History This was the first malt distillery to be owned by DCL. Sold in late 1988 to the Knockdhu Distillery Company Ltd. Two stills.

Geography Sited to the west of the B9022, seven miles north of Huntly.

Notes Built of local grey granite. The water supply, owned by the company, is supplied also to the villagers of Knock. It was occupied by a unit of the Indian Army from 1940 to 1945. The distillery was closed when purchased by its new owners but it re-opened in February 1989

Water A spring on the southern slopes of Knock Hill.

Age/Strength *12 YEARS 43% abv*
Tasting Notes
Degree of: Sweetness: ❾ Peatiness: ❸ Availability: ❹
Colour Straw with yellow highlights and a tinge of green
Nose Fresh, medium-bodied, malty and medium-sweet with a touch of greenness
Flavour Sweet, round, quite full-bodied and lightly peated
Finish Long, smooth and sweet with a green smokiness
Notes Inver House bottling. The malt produced by Knockdhu has changed its name to *An Cnoc* during 1993 because of confusion with another whisky

Age/Strength *1974 DISTILLATION 40% abv*
Tasting Notes
Degree of: Sweetness: ❾ Peatiness: ❸ Availability: ❹
Colour Pale straw/gold with yellow highlights
Nose Fatty, slightly sweet, quite full
Flavour Sweet, malty, slightly peppery
Finish Quite long, slightly oily
Notes Gordon and MacPhail bottling as Knockdhu

Ardbeg I

Distillery	Ardbeg
Established	1794
Address	Port Ellen, Islay, Argyll
Map Ref.	NR 414462
Distillery No.	107

The MASTER of Malt

ARDBEG
18 years old
SINGLE ISLAY MALT WHISKY

Distilled 9th August 1974
Bottled November 1992
A limited edition bottling from cask nos. 3445/6/7

Situated on the windswept southern coast of Islay, Ardbeg was established in 1794. The water source for this full, rich, peaty malt is Lochs Arinambeast and Uigidale.

70cl   Produce of Scotland   **43% vol**
Bottled exclusively in Scotland for The Master of Malt

History	The original distillery was run by a somewhat notorious band of smugglers, before Excisemen overran the place, destroying the buildings. John McDougall established the present distillery in 1815. Owned by Hiram Walker, itself now part of Allied Lyons, since 1979. It is operated by Caledonian Malt Whisky Distillers.
Geography	A very romantic, lonely site at the water's edge on the south coast of Islay.
Water	Supply from Lochs Arinambeast and Uigidale.

Age/Strength	*10 YEARS 40% abv*
Tasting Notes	
Degree of:	Sweetness: ❶ Peatiness: ❿ Availability: ❹
Colour	Pale straw with golden reflections
Nose	Peaty with an unusual sweet edge
Flavour	Full, peaty, rich with no hint of the sweetness indicated by the nose
Finish	Long and smoky
Notes	This was the company's own bottling

Age/Strength	*18 YEARS 43% abv*
Tasting Notes	
Degree of:	Sweetness: ❶ Peatiness: ❿ Availability: ❷
Colour	Mid-amber with old gold highlights
Nose	Full, pungent, very dry and smoky with a burnt oak character
Flavour	Big, burnt, very smoky, dry, peaty and oaky
Finish	Long, smoky and smooth with great pungency
Notes	Master of Malt bottling

Ardmore H

Distillery	Ardmore
Established	1898
Address	Kennethmont, Aberdeenshire
Map Ref.	NJ 553292
Distillery No.	62

History Built by Wm. Teacher with two stills and doubled in size twice - four stills in 1955 and eight stills in 1974. The distillery was built as part of a major expansion programme for the company's popular blended whiskies. Now operated by Caledonian Malt Whisky Distillers, part of Allied Lyons.

Geography Situated alongside the Aberdeen to Inverness railway, below the 1,425 ft Knockandy Hill. Close by is Leith Hall.

Notes Wm. Teacher use the make in blending "Highland Cream".

Water Spring on Knockandy Hill.

Age/Strength *15 YEARS 45.7% abv*

Tasting Notes

Degree of: Sweetness: ❽ Peatiness: ❼ Availability: ❶

Colour Very dark with rich deep amber highlights

Nose Full, rich, medium-sweet with a distinctive syrupy peatiness

Flavour Full, rich, sweet, complex flavours develop in the mouth - dry treacle, leafiness, burnt heather

Finish Spicy, vegetal greenness and dry, quite rich though

Notes Bottled by Wm. Teacher Limited. Limited supplies available

Age/Strength *18 YEARS 46% abv*

Tasting Notes

Degree of: Sweetness: ❽ Peatiness: ❻ Availability: ❹

Colour Full amber with golden highlights

Nose Light, slightly sweet and oaky

Flavour Malty, richly sweet and full

Finish Very fine, creamy and oaky

Notes Wm. Cadenhead bottling

Auchentoshan

Distillery	Auchentoshan
Established	c. 1800
Address	Dalmuir, Dunbartonshire
Map Ref.	NS 478726
Distillery No.	95

History The name Auchentoshan is believed to be derived from the Gaelic words "achadh oisnin" possibly meaning "corner of the field". Not much is known of the distillery's early years, but a Mr. Thorne has been recorded as owning it in 1825. It is now one of three distilleries owned by Morrison Bowmore Distillers. Although not the only distillery to experience war damage (see Banff) it had the misfortune to suffer heavily from enemy bombing, an event which caused extensive damage and a great loss of spirit!

Geography The distillery is situated next to the Erskine Bridge overlooking the River Clyde.

Notes Although geographically situated south of the Highland line, the source of Auchentoshan's water supply is north of the line. Thus the distillery is a Lowland one but its water supply is Highland. The make is triple distilled and very lightly peated. The first distillation takes an hour, the second five and the third nine hours.

Water Near Cochna Loch in the Kilpatrick Hills.

Age/Strength	*10 YEARS 40% abv*
Tasting Notes	
Degree of:	Sweetness: **4** Peatiness: **4** Availability: **4**
Colour	Very pale straw, slight green edge
Nose	Fresh, clean, floral aroma
Flavour	Light, soft, sweet and slightly fruity
Finish	Quite good but light

Aultmore S

Distillery	Aultmore
Established	1895
Address	Keith, Banffshire
Map Ref.	NJ 401534
Distillery No.	30

History	Built by Alexander Edward of Sanquhar, Forres with two stills. The first of the make was produced in early 1897. It became part of DCL in 1925 and transferred to SMD in 1930. Rebuilt in 1970/71 and doubled to four stills. Now part of United Distillers plc.
Geography	An isolated building standing on the A96 Keith to Elgin road close to the turning to Buckie.
Notes	Until 1969 a steam engine had been providing power, operating 24 hours a day, seven days a week since 1898. The old engine is still kept for show.
Water	The burn of Auchinderran.

Age/Strength	*12 YEARS 40% abv*
Tasting Notes	
Degree of:	Sweetness: ❺ Peatiness: ❹ Availability: ❶
Colour	Pale golden
Nose	Fresh, lightly peated and slightly sweet
Flavour	Medium-bodied, slightly fruity
Finish	Light and warming
Notes	DCL bottling

Age/Strength	*12 YEARS 43% abv*
Tasting Notes	
Degree of:	Sweetness: ❺ Peatiness: ❹ Availability: ❻
Colour	Pale straw with lemon highlights
Nose	Rich, round, medium-bodied, a cooked mash character, appley and spirity
Flavour	Medium-bodied, lightly peated and medium-dry
Finish	Smooth, malty and quite long
Notes	United Distillers bottling

Balblair

Distillery	Balblair
Established	1790
Address	Edderton, Ross-shire
Map Ref.	NH 706855
Distillery No.	5

History The present distillery was built in 1872, when the then owner, Andrew Ross, decided to extend the business, the new buildings being higher up the slope of the hill. The older buildings were converted into a bonded warehouse. Extended from two to three stills in the 1970s by owners Hiram Walker, now part of Allied Lyons. Operated by Caledonian Malt Whisky Distillers. The fermenting of ale on the site is said to have taken place as long ago as 1749.

Geography Less than a quarter of a mile from the Dornoch Firth, about six miles from Tain on the A9.

Notes Distilling in the area predates Balblair by more than a century, there being many suitable sources of water and peat in abundance. Indeed, the Edderton area is known as the "Parish of Peats" and once abounded in smuggling bothies. One of the malts associated with Ballantine's blended Scotch Whisky.

Water The Ault Dreag, a burn four miles from the distillery.

Age/Strength *5 YEARS 40% abv*

Tasting Notes

Degree of: Sweetness: **6** Peatiness: **4** Availability: **5**

Colour Very pale straw

Nose Peaty, aromatic, quite light and spirity

Flavour Slightly sweet, faintly peaty, spirity and quite light

Finish Shortish and light

Notes Gordon and MacPhail bottling

Age/Strength *10 YEARS 57% abv*

Tasting Notes

Degree of: Sweetness: **7** Peatiness: **4** Availability: **4**

Colour Quite deep amber with deep gold highlights

Nose Slightly musty, quite full with a sherry nuttiness but a dry nuttiness and hint of marzipan

Flavour Medium-sweet, oaky, full-bodied, slightly creamy and quite

Finish Long, spirity and spicy with characters of wood

Notes Gordon and MacPhail bottling

Balmenach

Distillery	Balmenach
Established	1824
Address	Cromdale, Moray
Map Ref.	NJ 078271
Distillery No.	66

History | The distillery was established in 1824 by James McGregor. At the time it was at the centre of an area which was full of smugglers' bothies and illicit distilling was a way of life. Bought by SMD in 1930 and extended from four stills to six stills in 1962, it is now part of United Distillers plc. Closed May 1993.

Geography | The distillery lies in a bowl in the hills off the A95 main road heading towards Bridge of Avon from Grantown-on-Spey.

Notes | The distillery stands about a mile from the former Cromdale station on the Spey Valley line. A branch line was built to the distillery in the late 1880s and the steam engine which worked the line is preserved on the Strathspey railway at Aviemore.

Water | The Cromdale Burn.

SPEYSIDE
SINGLE MALT
SCOTCH WHISKY

Sometime in the early 19th, after *walking* in the *CROMDALE* hills *with* his 2 BROTHERS, *James McGregor* settled and established

BALMENACH

distillery. Spring water from beneath those *same HILLS* is still used to produce this *RICH flavoured single MALT SCOTCH WHISKY* of *exemplary* quality.

A G E D 12 Y E A R S

43% vol   Distilled & Bottled in *SCOTLAND*.
BALMENACH DISTILLERY, Cromdale, Moray, Scotland.   70 cl

Age/Strength	*12 YEARS 43% abv*
Tasting Notes	
Degree of:	Sweetness: ❼ Peatiness: ❺ Availability: ❻
Colour	Quite deep amber with bronze highlights
Nose	Quite full-bodied, heather floral characters, medium-sweet rich and sherried with a light honeyed nuttiness
Flavour	Full-bodied, sherried and nutty with a touch of oily vanilla
Finish	Long, nutty and medium-sweet with a touch of tannin
Notes	United Distillers bottling

Balmenach

Age/Strength	*1971 DISTILLATION 40% abv*
Tasting Notes	
Degree of:	Sweetness: **5** Peatiness: **7** Availability: **4**
Colour	Amber/straw with yellow/gold highlights
Nose	Quite smoky and peaty, medium-bodied, with slight green nuttiness
Flavour	Dryish, smoky, quite full and delicately peaty with an edge of sweetness
Finish	Dry with oaky tannin and reasonable length
Notes	Gordon & MacPhail bottling

Age/Strength	*1970 DISTILLATION 40% abv*
Tasting Notes	
Degree of:	Sweetness: **5** Peatiness: **6** Availability: **4**
Colour	Straw/golden
Nose	Light but faintly sweet
Flavour	Much bigger than the nose suggests, a little woody and with a pleasant sweet edge
Finish	Full and distinguished
Notes	Gordon & MacPhail bottling

BALMENACH DISTILLERY

The Balvenie

Distillery	Balvenie
Established	1892
Address	Dufftown, Banffshire
Map Ref.	NJ 324414
Distillery No.	52

History	Built next to William Grant's Glenfiddich distillery in 1892. The stills came second-hand from Lagavulin and Glen Albyn. Three further stills were added to make eight in all (two in 1965 and one in 1971).
Geography	Situated just below Glenfiddich on the lower slopes of the Convals, the hills which dominate Dufftown.
Notes	The Balvenie is an excellent example of just how different single malts can be. Standing next door to its more famous sister, Glenfiddich, it draws its water from the same source and shares the same supply of malt - and yet the two whiskies are very different in character.
Water	The Robbie Dubh (pronounced "doo") spring.

Age/Strength	*10 YEARS 40% abv*
Tasting Notes	
Degree of:	Sweetness: **9** Peatiness: **3** Availability: **9**
Colour	Straw with good golden highlights
Nose	Full, rich with a green edge, medium-sweet, apples
Flavour	Medium-dry, smooth, oaky, malty
Finish	Reasonable length, quite rich
Notes	William Grant bottling

Age/Strength	*NO AGE STATEMENT 40% abv*
Tasting Notes	
Degree of:	Sweetness: **9** Peatiness: **3** Availability: **5**
Colour	Pale golden
Nose	Full, richly powerful and aromatic
Flavour	Big-bodied, sweet and gloriously malty
Finish	Long and with a strange sweet aftertaste
Notes	William Grant bottling

Banff

Distillery	Banff
Established	1863
Address	Banff, Banffshire
Map Ref.	NJ 668643

History Built by James Simpson junior, to replace an earlier distillery of the same name built in 1824. Rebuilt after a fire in 1877. Owned by SMD since 1932. Two stills.

Geography Half a mile west of Banff on the B9139.

Notes One of the earliest distilleries to be located in order to take advantage of the railways, although Banff's rail connection has long since been axed. On Saturday, 16th August 1941 a single German plane machine-gunned and bombed No. 12 warehouse. Exploding whisky casks flew through the air and a local paper said, "Thousands of gallons of whisky were lost, either burning or running to waste over the land... even farm animals became intoxicated." It is said that cows were not milked because they could not be got to their feet. Now closed.

Water Springs on Fiskaidly Farm.

Age/Strength *1974 DISTILLATION 40% abv*

Tasting Notes

Degree of: Sweetness: **❿** Peatiness: **❻** Availability: **❹**

Colour Medium-peaty gold

Nose Quite peaty, slightly oily with a hint of ozone

Flavour Sweet, round, mellow, slightly spicy

Finish Good, long, slightly sugary-sweet, a little overpoweringly so

Notes Gordon & MacPhail bottling

BANFF DISTILLERY

Ben Nevis

Distillery	Ben Nevis
Established	1825
Address	Lochy Bridge, Fort William, Inverness-shire
Map Ref.	NN 126757
Distillery No.	74
History	Founded by "Long John" Macdonald in 1825. Owned by

DISTILLED AND BOTTLED IN SCOTLAND

BEN NEVIS

SINGLE HIGHLAND MALT SCOTCH WHISKY

BEN NEVIS DISTILLERY (FORT WILLIAM) LIMITED
DISTILLED IN 1966

75cl   ウイスキー   59%vol

	various Macdonalds until bought by Seager Evans Ltd in the 1920s. Taken over by Ben Nevis Distillery (Fort William) Ltd who installed a Coffey still. Four pot stills. Sold by the Whitbread group to the Japanese company, Nikka, early in 198
Geography	Situated two miles north of Fort William on the A82.
Notes	A cask of Ben Nevis was presented to Queen Victoria on her visit to Fort William in 1848. The cask was not to be opened unt the Prince of Wales attained his majority 15 years later.
Water	Buchan's Well on Ben Nevis.

Age/Strength	*1972 DISTILLATION 60.5% abv*
Tasting Notes	
Degree of:	Sweetness: ❺ Peatiness: ❻ Availability: ❹
Colour	Pale amber with gold highlights
Nose	Medium-sweet, quite rich and fresh with a touch of oily oaky vanilla, a green character and medium-bodied
Flavour	Medium-sweet, smoky and smooth with a little tannin and a green freshness
Finish	Long, gently smoky with a touch of spice
Notes	Cask sample - to be bottled shortly at cask strength, cask no. 61

Age/Strength	*22 YEARS 46% abv*
Tasting Notes	
Degree of:	Sweetness: ❸ Peatiness: ❻ Availability: ❹
Colour	Deep peaty amber with good gold highlights
Nose	Spirity, malty, dryish, lightly peated, slightly leafy
Flavour	Dry, lightly peaty, spirity, slightly spicy
Finish	Smooth, clean and enjoyably long
Notes	Wm. Cadenhead bottling

Benriach S

Distillery	Benriach
Established	1898
Address	Longmorn, nr. Elgin, Moray
Map Ref.	NJ 230585
Distillery No.	19
History	Founded in 1898 as the whisky market moved into recession. It was then closed in 1900 and did not open until 1965, when it was rebuilt by The Glenlivet Distillers Ltd. Owned by The Seagram Company of Canada since 1977. Four stills.
Geography	Situated three miles south of Elgin to the east of the A941.
Notes	The floor maltings are still in use.
Water	Local springs.

CONNOISSEURS CHOICE

Connoisseurs Choice, a range of single malts from various districts of Scotland.

The distilleries situated in the area of the valley of the River Spey produce some of the finest malt whiskies.

SINGLE SPEYSIDE
MALT SCOTCH WHISKY
DISTILLED AT
BENRIACH
DISTILLERY
PROPRIETORS: The Longmorn-Glenlivet Distilleries Ltd
DISTILLED 1982 DISTILLED
SPECIALLY SELECTED, PRODUCED AND BOTTLED BY
70cl GORDON & MACPHAIL 40%vol
ELGIN · SCOTLAND
PRODUCT OF SCOTLAND

Age/Strength	*1970 DISTILLATION 40% abv*
Tasting Notes	
Degree of:	Sweetness: ❼ Peatiness: ❸ Availability: ❹
Colour	Bright amber with good, greeny/gold highlights
Nose	Rich, fresh, slightly green citrusy and medium-sweet with a floral touch and hint of toffee
Flavour	Quite full, fruity, nutty and round with a touch of greenness
Finish	Smooth, quite long and apple fruity
Notes	Gordon and MacPhail bottling

Age/Strength	*1969 DISTILLATION 40% abv*
Tasting Notes	
Degree of:	Sweetness: ❽ Peatiness: ❸ Availability: ❹
Colour	Pale straw with gold highlights
Nose	Sweet, distinctive fruitiness, fresh and appley
Flavour	Sweet, appley, distinctive, reminiscent of Calvados
Finish	Spicy, good with the apple flavour lingering
Notes	Gordon and MacPhail bottling

Benrinnes S

Distillery	Benrinnes
Established	1835
Address	Aberlour, Banffshire
Map Ref.	NJ 259397
Distillery No.	48
History	The original distillery was located at Whitehouse Farm, three quarters of a mile to the south east and was washed away in the great flood of 1829. The present distillery was founded in 1835 by William Smith & Company as an extension of the farmsteading. Acquired by Dewar's in 1922 thereby becoming a part of DCL in 1925. Run by SMD since 1930. Doubled from three to six stills in 1966. Major reconstruction took place between 1955 and 1956. Now part of United Distillers plc.
Geography	Situated on a loop of an unclassified road, one and half miles south of the A95, between it and the B9009.
Notes	A form of triple distillation is practised.
Water	The Scurran and Rowantree Burns.

Age/Strength	*15 YEARS 43% abv*
Tasting Notes	
Degree of:	Sweetness: ❽ Peatiness: ❹ Availability: ❻
Colour	Amber with old gold highlights
Nose	Medium-bodied, biscuity-yeasty, fresh, vanilla and medium-sweet with a slight floral note
Flavour	Medium-sweet, round, biscuity and honeyed
Finish	Nice sweet, round, biscuity and honeyed
Notes	United Distillers bottling

Age/Strength	*1968 DISTILLATION 40% abv*
Tasting Notes	
Degree of:	Sweetness: ❽ Peatiness: ❻ Availability: ❹
Colour	Straw/gold with good bright highlights
Nose	Sweet, nutty, slightly fatty
Flavour	Medium-sweet, smoky, spicy, oaky
Finish	Good, smoky and dry, smooth and creamy
Notes	Gordon & MacPhail bottling

Benromach

Distillery	Benromach
Established	1898
Address	Forres, Moray
Map Ref.	NJ 033593
Distillery No.	22

CONNOISSEURS CHOICE

Connoisseurs Choice, a range of single malts from various districts of Scotland.

In the Highlands are situated the greatest number of malt whisky distilleries.

SINGLE HIGHLAND
MALT SCOTCH WHISKY
DISTILLED AT
BENROMACH
DISTILLERY
Proprietors: J. & W. Hardie Ltd.
DISTILLED 1971 DISTILLED
SPECIALLY SELECTED, PRODUCED AND BOTTLED BY
70cl   GORDON & MACPHAIL   40%vol
ELGIN · SCOTLAND
PRODUCT OF SCOTLAND

History	Built by the Benromach Distillery Company. Bought by DCL in 1953 and transferred to SMD. Rebuilt in 1966 and again in 1974. Two stills.
Geography	Sited to the north of Forres on the north side of the railway.
Notes	In 1925 the mash tun was wooden. Benromach has high pitched gables and narrow mullioned windows in the Scots vernacular style of the 17th century. Closed but recently sold to Gordon and MacPhail who have plans to re-open it.
Water	Chapeltown springs near Forres.

Age/Strength	*1969 DISTILLATION 40% abv*
Tasting Notes	
Degree of:	Sweetness: ❼ Peatiness: ❺ Availability: ❹
Colour	Mid-amber with yellow/gold highlights
Nose	Fresh and medium-dry with an oily-oaky aroma; soft and smooth with a touch of green apples
Flavour	Medium-dry, quite rich and soft, sweetness develops in the palate, gently peated
Finish	Quite long and lightly smoky with a touch of spice on the tail
Notes	Gordon and MacPhail bottling

Age/Strength	*1968 DISTILLATION 40% abv*
Tasting Notes	
Degree of:	Sweetness: ❽ Peatiness: ❹ Availability: ❹
Colour	Deepish amber, slightly grey-green tints
Nose	Full, ripe, sweet and definitely fruity
Flavour	Sweet, mellow, soft, a little spirity
Finish	Spicy and long and with a little touch of a floral note
Notes	Gordon & MacPhail bottling

Bladnoch

Distillery	Bladnoch
Established	1817
Address	Bladnoch, Wigtown
Map Ref.	NX 421543
Distillery No.	115

LOWLAND
SINGLE MALT
SCOTCH WHISKY

The *Broad Leaved Helleborine*,
a rare species of *wild orchid*, can be found growing
in the *ancient oak woodland* behind the

BLADNOCH

distillery. The most southerly in *SCOTLAND*,
founded in the early 1800's, & the
distillery stands by the *RIVER BLADNOCH*
near *Wigtown*. It produces a *distinctive*
LOWLAND single MALT WHISKY – delicate and
fruity with a *lemony* aroma and *taste*.

A G E D **10** Y E A R S

43% vol   Distilled & Bottled in *SCOTLAND*   70 cl
BLADNOCH DISTILLERY, Bladnoch, Wigtownshire, Scotland

History	Founded in 1817 by John and Thomas McClelland. Closed in 1938 and re-opened in 1956. Extended from two to four stills in 1966. Part of United Distillers plc who have tried unsuccessfully to sell it.
Geography	The southernmost distillery in Scotland. Situated on the river of the same name just a mile outside Wigtown.
Notes	Close to the distillery is Baldoon Farm, where stands the ruined castle to which Janet Dalrymple, the "Bride of Lammermoor" came to die after her marriage to David Dunbar of Baldoon. The distillery closed in May 1993.
Water	The river Bladnoch.

Age/Strength	*8 YEARS 40% abv*
Tasting Notes	
Degree of:	Sweetness: **❶** Peatiness: **❹** Availability: **❻**
Colour	Light amber
Nose	Very light, dry
Flavour	Light, delicate and dry
Finish	Slightly spirity, but lasts well

Age/Strength	*10 YEARS 43% abv*
Tasting Notes	
Degree of:	Sweetness: **❹** Peatiness: **❹** Availability: **❻**
Colour	Straw/amber with yellow highlights and a slight green tinge
Nose	Fresh, quite full and fruity and floral, medium-dry with an attractive grape spirit-like aroma
Flavour	Fresh with good weight and edge of sweetness and a touch of spice
Finish	Fresh with nice sweetness and quite light
Notes	United Distillers bottling

Blair Athol **H**

Distillery	Blair Athol
Established	1798
Address	Pitlochry, Perthshire
Map Ref.	NN 946577
Distillery No.	79

HIGHLAND
SINGLE MALT
SCOTCH WHISKY

BLAIR ATHOL

distillery, established in 1798, stands
on *peaty moorland* in the *foothills* of the
GRAMPIAN MOUNTAINS. An ancient
source of water for the *distillery, ALLT
DOUR BURN* - 'The *Burn of the Otter',*
flows close by. This *single MALT
SCOTCH WHISKY* has a mellow deep
toned aroma, a *strong fruity*
flavour and a smooth finish.

A G E D 12 Y E A R S

43% vol   70 cl

History Although originally founded almost 30 years earlier, the present distillery was established in 1826 when revived by John Robertson. It passed into the hands of Alexander Conacher and Company in 1827. It closed in 1932 and although purchased the following year by Arthur Bell and Sons, it did not come to life again until 1949 when it was rebuilt. Extended from two to four stills in 1973. Now part of United Distillers plc.

Geography Not at Blair Athol as its name suggests. It is to be found on the southern approach road to Pitlochry, just off the new A9.

Notes The distillery has a large modern visitor centre. The Conacher family, who owned the distillery for a time in the 1800s, are said to be descended from the chivalrous young Conacher who so admired Catherine Glover, the fair Maid of Perth.

Water From a spring on the nearby 2,760 ft Ben Vrackie.

Age/Strength *8 YEARS 40% abv*
Tasting Notes
Degree of: Sweetness: **8** Peatiness: **5** Availability: **2**
Colour Straw / golden
Nose Fresh, clean and lightly peated
Flavour Sweet, almost almondy
Finish Quite good and distinctive

Age/Strength *12 YEARS 43% abv*
Tasting Notes
Degree of: Sweetness: **7** Peatiness: **6** Availability: **6**
Colour Pale, mid-amber with good highlights
Nose Quite full with touches of nuttiness and greenness, medium-sweet with a fresh smokiness
Flavour Medium-sweet and quite full, spicy and round with a definite smoky tang
Finish Fresh, quite long and smoky with sweetness on the tail

Bowmore

Distillery	Bowmore
Established	1779
Address	Bowmore, Islay
Map Ref.	NR 309599
Distillery No.	106

History In 1776, an Islay merchant, David Simpson, obtained permission from the local Laird to build dwellings and "other buildings". The "other buildings" were soon converted to a distillery. Bought by Stanley P. Morrison in 1963. Now owned by Morrison Bowmore Distillers.

Geography Bowmore stands, almost fortress-like, on the shores of Loch Indaal.

Notes Uses a revolutionary waste heat recovery system to cut costs. The distillery was built early in the village's history at the foot o Hill Street and has proved important to its economic survival. Said to be the oldest legal distillery on the island.

Water Laggan River.

Age/Strength *10 YEARS 40% abv*
Tasting Notes
Degree of: Sweetness: ❶ Peatiness: ❾ Availability: ❾
Colour Mid-amber with gold highlights
Nose Full, dry, pungent with a touch of burnt heather and perfume
Flavour Dry, heather-perfumed, fresh and smoky, quite full-bodied wit whiffs of ozone
Finish Long, characterful and smoky

Age/Strength *12 YEARS 40% abv*
Tasting Notes
Degree of: Sweetness: ❶ Peatiness: ❾ Availability: ❾
Colour Full, amber, very bright
Nose Lightish, peaty, burnt heather, characteristic tang of ozone/ iodine and even a whiff of chocolate
Flavour Smooth, refined flavour with a pronounced peatiness
Finish A good long dry finish

Bowmore

Age/Strength	*BOWMORE "LEGEND" 40% abv*
Tasting Notes	
Degree of:	Sweetness: **❶** Peatiness: **❾** Availability: **❽**
Colour	Light amber with gold highlights and a tinge of green
Nose	Full, pungent, a touch perfumed and a little greenness
Flavour	Dry with an edge of richness, perfumed and quite pungent
Finish	Long, gently smoky and perfumed

Age/Strength	*21 YEARS 43% abv*
Tasting Notes	
Degree of:	Sweetness: **❷** Peatiness: **❾** Availability: **❻**
Colour	Mid-amber with old gold highlights
Nose	Quite big-bodied, dark and smoky, rounded and quite dry with just a hint of ozone
Flavour	Big, round, burnt heather roots, quite pungent with a delicate floral note at the back
Finish	Long with a hint of sweetness/richness, finely smoky with a touch of bitter chocolate on the tail

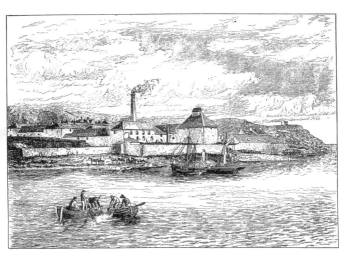

BOWMORE DISTILLERY

Brora

Distillery	Brora
Established	1819
Address	Brora, Sutherland
Map Ref.	NC 897053
Distillery No.	4
Notes	Brora was known as Clynelish until 1969. After the modern distillery had been built in 1967-68, the old "Clynelish" re-opened in April 1969, housed in the rebuilt old Brora mash house. It subsequently ceased distillation in May 1983.
Water	Clynemilton Burn.

Age/Strength	*1972 DISTILLATION 40% abv*
Tasting Notes	
Degree of:	Sweetness: ❸ Peatiness: ❾ Availability: ❷
Colour	Mid-amber with gold highlights
Nose	Full, big-bodied and quite heavily peated with a sooty character
Flavour	Big and smooth with smoky characters of burnt oak
Finish	Nutty, chewy with a hint of sweetness
Notes	Gordon and MacPhail bottling

Bruichladdich

Distillery	Bruichladdich
Established	1881
Address	Bruichladdich, Islay
Map Ref.	NR 264612
Distillery No.	105
History	Built by Robert, William and John Gourlay Harvey (of the Dundashill and Yoker Harveys). Became the Bruichladdich Distillery Company (Islay) Ltd in 1886.
Geography	Doubled from two to four stills in 1975. Sited on the western side of the island.
Notes	The distillery is the most westerly in Scotland and this is thought to have a bearing on the lighter flavour it has compared with other Islay malts.
Water	A reservoir in the local hills.

Bruichladdich

Age/Strength	*10 YEARS 40% abv*
Tasting Notes	
Degree of:	Sweetness: ❷ Peatiness: ❼ Availability: ❼
Colour	Pale golden with slight green tinges
Nose	A delicate peatiness, fairly light with no great pungency
Flavour	Full and flavoursome, smoky and dry, without the heavy notes of other Islays
Finish	Good length with a well defined finish

Age/Strength	*15 YEARS 40% abv*
Tasting Notes	
Degree of:	Sweetness: ❸ Peatiness: ❻ Availability: ❹
Colour	Straw with amber-gold highlights
Nose	Rich, delicately peated, with underlying sweetness
Flavour	Slightly sweet with hints of nuttiness and very little of Islay's characteristics
Finish	Spicy, warm, long with sweet oak, but finally dry

Age/Strength	*21 YEARS 43% abv*
Tasting Notes	
Degree of:	Sweetness: ❸ Peatiness: ❻ Availability: ❻
Colour	Light amber with yellow/gold highlights
Nose	Quite light, fresh and rich with a faint touch of ozone
Flavour	Medium-bodied, fresh, almost dry, but with an edge of richness - an intriguing mixture of sweetness and dryness
Finish	Tangy, fresh, rich and clean and gently smoky

BRUICHLADDICH DISTILLERY, FROM THE SEA

Bunnahabhain I

Distillery	Bunnahabhain
Established	1880
Address	Near Port Askaig, Islay
Map Ref.	NR 420732
Distillery No.	91

"Westering Home"

Bunnahabhain
SINGLE ISLAY MALT SCOTCH WHISKY
PRODUCT OF SCOTLAND
THE BUNNAHABHAIN DISTILLERY COMPANY,
BUNNAHABHAIN, ISLE OF ISLAY, SCOTLAND. BOTTLED IN SCOTLAND
40% vol.   70cl

History	Became part of Highland Distilleries in 1887 when amalgamated with William Grant and Company of Glenrothes. Extended from two to four stills in 1963.
Geography	Situated towards the north east tip of Islay on the bay from which it takes its name.
Notes	Bunnahabhain means "mouth of the river". Prior to the building of this distillery, which is Islay's most northerly, the adjacent area was inhospitable and uninhabited. Now a small hamlet has built up around the distillery.
Water	River Margadale.

Age/Strength	*12 YEARS 40% abv*
Tasting Notes	
Degree of:	Sweetness: ❸ Peatiness: ❼ Availability: ❽
Colour	Straw with golden highlights
Nose	Distinctive, quite light and flowery
Flavour	Smoother, softer and less pungent than other Islays
Finish	Lovely, round and long

Age/Strength	*1964 DISTILLATION 25 YEARS 46% abv*
Tasting Notes	
Degree of:	Sweetness: ❺ Peatiness: ❻ Availability: ❶
Colour	Straw with yellow highlights
Nose	Medium-sweet, rich, ripe and fruity with a dark tarriness at the back and a floral note
Flavour	Medium-sweet and rich with oaky tannins; quite smooth and creamy
Finish	Rich, full-bodied and quite long with an earthy smokiness on the tail
Notes	Master of Malt bottling cask no. 4852-6

Bushmills Malt IR

Distillery	Bushmills
Established	1608
Address	Co. Antrim, N. Ireland
Map Ref.	East 9347 North 4052

History | Bushmills was granted a licence to distil in 1608, making it by far the earliest legal distillery of all. Operated by Irish Distillers which in 1988 was the target of a hard fought takeover battle between the British giant Grand Metropolitan and French rival Pernod Ricard, which the latter won.

Geography | Situated on the north coast of Ulster, close to the Giant's Causeway.

Notes | Bushmills is triple distilled, a fact which is widely advertised, although it is not alone in this respect. The Scottish malts Auchentoshan, Benrinnes and Rosebank are also triple distilled. Bushmills is also available in duty-free markets at 43% abv.

Water | Saint Columb's Rill.

Age/Strength | *10 YEARS 40% abv*

Tasting Notes

Degree of: Sweetness: ❻ Peatiness: ❶ Availability: ❾

Colour | Deep amber with gold reflections

Nose | Slightly oily, grassy, gooseberries, very slightly smoky

Flavour | Delicately sweet, quite complex, round, mellow, slightly spicy

Finish | Long, fine and almost vinous or grapey

Caol Ila

Distillery	Caol Ila
Established	1846
Address	Port Askaig, Islay
Map Ref.	NR 433695
Distillery No.	103

ISLAY
SINGLE MALT *SCOTCH WHISKY*

CAOL ILA

*distillery, built in 1846 is situated near Port Askaig on the Isle of Islay.
Steamers used to call twice a week to collect whisky from this remote
site in a cove facing the Isle of Jura. Water supplies for mashing
come from Loch nam Ban although the sea provides water for
condensing. Unusual for an Islay this single MALT SCOTCH
WHISKY has a fresh aroma and a light yet well rounded flavour.*

AGED 15 YEARS

43% vol Distilled & Bottled in SCOTLAND CAOL ILA DISTILLERY Port Askaig, Isle of Islay, Scotland 70 cl

History	Built by Hector Henderson. Extended and rebuilt by Bulloch, Lade & Company in 1879. Came under the control of the DCL in 1927 and transferred to SMD three years later. The premises were completely rebuilt, apart from the warehouses, between April 1972 and January 1974 when extended from two to six stills.
Geography	Almost literally at the end of the road - the northern end of the A846.
Notes	"Caol Ila" is the Gaelic name for the Sound of Islay, the strait that separates Islay from Jura. Hot water from the distillery is pumped through sea water condensers, cooled and returned for re-use.
Water	Loch Nam Ban (Torrbolls Loch).

Age/Strength	*12 YEARS 63% abv*
Tasting Notes	
Degree of:	Sweetness: **5** Peatiness: **9** Availability: **2**
Colour	Amber-peaty with good gold highlights
Nose	Peaty, burnt heather, quite earthy, medicinal
Flavour	Medium-sweet, rich smoky, spicy, full burnt heather
Finish	Smooth, smoky, spicy, very long
Notes	Sherry cask bottling from James MacArthur & Company. The richness derives from the sherry casks used for ageing

Age/Strength	*15 YEARS 43% abv*
Tasting Notes	
Degree of:	Sweetness: **2** Peatiness: **9** Availability: **6**
Colour	Straw/pale amber with lemon yellow highlights
Nose	Full, quite pungent and peaty, smoky, burnt heather roots with a touch of unripe greenness
Flavour	Big, full, smoky and pungent with an edge of sweetness
Finish	Long, rich, smoky with a touch of chocolate and spice
Notes	United Distillers bottling

Caol Ila

Age/Strength	*17 YEARS 43% abv*
Tasting Notes	
Degree of:	Sweetness: ❶ Peatiness: ❾ Availability: ❷
Colour	Pale amber with a tinge of lemony/gold
Nose	Full-bodied, rich, round and nutty, medium pungency, soft peatiness, quite dry
Flavour	Dry, smoky, pungent and full-bodied
Finish	Long and smoky
Notes	Master of Malt bottling - cask nos. 12442-12446

Age/Strength	*18 YEARS 43% abv*
Tasting Notes	
Degree of:	Sweetness: ❶ Peatiness: ❾ Availability: ❷
Colour	Very pale straw with lemon highlights
Nose	Full-bodied, pungent and dry with the aroma of burnt heather roots
Flavour	Full, pungent, smoky and dry with just a hint of sweetness on the edge
Finish	Long, characterful and smoky with oaky tannins
Notes	Master of Malt bottling cask nos. 10/12

Age/Strength	*1974 DISTILLATION 40% abv*
Tasting Notes	
Degree of:	Sweetness: ❷ Peatiness: ❾ Availability: ❹
Colour	Bright gold/amber with gold highlights
Nose	Peaty, malty, earthy, more than a hint of the sea, but with a rich, full, almost perfumed fruitiness to it
Flavour	Dry, round, quite full-bodied and peaty
Finish	Long, smoky and dry, but rich
Notes	Gordon and MacPhail bottling

Age/Strength	*1972 DISTILLATION 40% abv*
Tasting Notes	
Degree of:	Sweetness: ❷ Peatiness: ❾ Availability: ❹
Colour	Palish gold with green tinges
Nose	Peaty, almost medicinal, strange touch of sweetness
Flavour	Heavy, clean, peaty, burnt heather with more than a tang of ozone
Finish	Long, distinguished and smoky
Notes	Gordon and MacPhail bottling

Caperdonich

Distillery	Caperdonich
Established	1897
Address	Rothes, Moray
Map Ref.	NJ 278496
Distillery No.	34

CONNOISSEURS CHOICE

Connoisseurs Choice, a range of single malts from various districts of Scotland

The distilleries situated in the area of the valley of the River Spey produce some of the finest malt whiskies.

SINGLE SPEYSIDE
MALT SCOTCH WHISKY
DISTILLED AT
CAPERDONICH
DISTILLERY
Proprietors: The Glenlivet & Glen Grant Distilleries Ltd
DISTILLED **1968** DISTILLED

SPECIALLY SELECTED, PRODUCED AND BOTTLED BY
70cl   **GORDON & MACPHAIL**   40%vol
ELGIN - SCOTLAND
PRODUCT OF SCOTLAND

History	Following the industry slump at the turn of the century, Caperdonich was closed in 1902 and did not produce again until 1965 following rebuilding. Extended from two to four stills in 1967. Now owned by The Seagram Company of Canada.
Geography	Situated across the road from its sister, Glen Grant.
Notes	The distillery was built to supplement the output of Glen Grant and was known as Glen Grant No. 2. The whisky, using the same water, is lighter and fruitier than Glen Grant. The two distilleries were originally joined by a pipe which carried spirit from Caperdonich to Glen Grant across the town's main street.
Water	The Caperdonich Well, adjacent to the Glen Grant Burn.

Age/Strength	*1979 DISTILLATION 40% abv*
Tasting Notes	
Degree of:	Sweetness: ❽ Peatiness: ❸ Availability: ❹
Colour	Pale straw. Almost yellow
Nose	Sweet, ripe, grapey with a hint of cloves and apples
Flavour	Sweet, slight flavour of cloves, spirity
Finish	Quite good for its youth, but shortish
Notes	Gordon & MacPhail bottling

Age/Strength	*1972 DISTILLATION 40% abv*
Tasting Notes	
Degree of:	Sweetness: ❼ Peatiness: ❸ Availability: ❷
Colour	Honey-amber with old gold highlights
Nose	Full, fruity, almost raisins, nutty and delicately peated with hint of demerara sugar
Flavour	Quite full and oaky with good peatiness, smooth, medium-sweet with hints of richness
Finish	Long, creamy and spicy with oaky tannins
Notes	Master of Malt bottling - cask nos. 7130-2

Caperdonich  S

Age/Strength	*1968 DISTILLATION 40% abv*
Tasting Notes	
Degree of:	Sweetness: ❼ Peatiness: ❸ Availability: ❹
Colour	Mid-amber with good, gold highlights
Nose	Light, delicate with medium-sweet richness, slightly appley and a touch of a floral note
Flavour	Medium-bodied, spicy, creamy smooth with a lanolin character
Finish	Fresh, medium-dry, clean
Notes	Gordon and MacPhail bottling

Cardhu S

Distillery	Cardhu
Established	1824
Address	Knockando, Moray
Map Ref.	NJ 191431
Distillery No.	34
History	Built on a farm known as Cardow and called until recently by that name. Acquired by John Walker and Son in 1893, becoming part of DCL in 1925. Transferred to SMD in 1930. Rebuilt in 1960 and extended from four to six stills. Now part of United Distillers plc.
Geography	Situated high up above the River Spey on its north side, on the B9102 between Knockando and Craigellachie.
Notes	A "flagship" of the United Distillers Group, the malt has long played an important role in Johnnie Walker's famous Red and Black Label brands. Cardhu means black rock. A very large reception centre was opened in 1988.
Water	Springs on the Mannoch Hill or the Lyne Burn.
Age/Strength	*12 YEARS 40% abv*
Tasting Notes	
Degree of:	Sweetness: ❽ Peatiness: ❼ Availability: ❾
Colour	Pale mid-amber with a definite green tinge
Nose	Quite full-bodied, rich, medium-sweet and smoky, appley
Flavour	Round and mellow; sweet with a delicate peatiness
Finish	Long, peaty and sweet

Clynelish

Distillery	Clynelish
Established	1967
Address	Brora, Sutherland
Map Ref.	NC 897053
Distillery No.	4

History	Now part of United Distillers plc. Six stills.
Geography	Just off the A9 at Brora.
Notes	Built next to the old "Clynelish" distillery (See also Brora). A new visitor centre opened in 1988.
Water	Clynemilton Burn.

Age/Strength	*12 YEARS 40% abv*
Tasting Notes	
Degree of:	Sweetness: ❹ Peatiness: ❻ Availability: ❷
Colour	Pale straw with lovely golden edges
Nose	Dry with a touch of sweetness on the edge. Slightly fruity and softly peated
Flavour	Full bodied, slightly creamy and spicy
Finish	Long, dry and smoky

Age/Strength	*14 YEARS 43% abv*
Tasting Notes	
Degree of:	Sweetness: ❹ Peatiness: ❻ Availability: ❻
Colour	Pale amber with good green/gold highlights
Nose	Rich, medium-dry, a citrus fruitiness, quite full and round with good smokiness at the back
Flavour	Smoky with soft sweetness, quite full-bodied and almost luscious - very complex
Finish	Long and elegant with a touch of bitter chocolate

Age/Strength	*1965 DISTILLATION 23 YEARS 51.7% abv*
Tasting Notes	
Degree of:	Sweetness: ❹ Peatiness: ❻ Availability: ❹
Colour	Pale amber with a touch of green; good yellow highlights
Nose	Full, fruity, herby, medium-dry with a touch of woodiness and high spiritiness
Flavour	Dry, but with a touch of sweetness, round, full, a slight oiliness and good fruit character
Finish	Long, nutty, spicy and very full - something of a blockbuster
Notes	Wm. Cadenhead bottling

48

Coleburn

Distillery	Coleburn
Established	1897
Address	Longmorn, Elgin, Moray
Map Ref.	NJ 240553
Distillery No.	20

CONNOISSEURS CHOICE

Connoisseurs Choice, a range of single malts from various distances of Scotland

The distilleries situated in the area of the valley of the River Spey produce some of the finest malt whiskies.

SINGLE SPEYSIDE
MALT SCOTCH WHISKY
DISTILLED AT
COLEBURN
DISTILLERY
Proprietors: J. & G. Stewart Ltd.
DISTILLED 1972 DISTILLED
SPECIALLY SELECTED, PRODUCED AND BOTTLED BY
70cl GORDON & MACPHAIL 40%vol
ELGIN - SCOTLAND
PRODUCT OF SCOTLAND

History	Built by John Robertson & Son. Became part of DCL in 1925 and transferred to SMD in 1930. Two stills.
Geography	Situated to the east of the A491, four miles south of Elgin. It is "faced on one side by a plantation of Scotch firs and birches, and swept by the cool mountain breezes of Brown Muir" according to Robertson's original announcement in 1896.
Notes	The distillery was built in warm-coloured Moray sandstone and roofed with blue Welsh slates. A problem which faced the architect was the provision of a lavatory to the Excise Office - it took 18 months to resolve! The Excise Officer's house took even longer to be completed. The distillery is now closed.
Water	A spring in the Glen of Rothes.

Age/Strength Tasting Notes | *1972 DISTILLATION 40% abv*

Degree of:	Sweetness: **7** Peatiness: **6** Availability: **4**
Colour	Straw/amber with yellow/gold highlights
Nose	Medium-bodied, quite heavily peated, fresh and nutty with a touch of greenness
Flavour	Medium-dry, smoky, quite heavy with a richness and unripe green character
Finish	Smoky with richness at back and light touches of oaky tannins
Notes	Gordon and MacPhail bottling

Age/Strength Tasting Notes | *1965 DISTILLATION 40% abv*

Degree of:	Sweetness: **8** Peatiness: **5** Availability: **4**
Colour	Warm peaty/gold with amber highlights
Nose	Sweet, nutty, almondy, oily rich
Flavour	Medium-sweet, delicate, slightly spirity, rich
Finish	Smooth and creamy with good length
Notes	Gordon and MacPhail bottling

Convalmore S

Distillery	Convalmore
Established	1893
Address	Dufftown, Banffshire
Map Ref.	NJ 322418
Distillery No.	49

CONNOISSEURS
CHOICE

Connoisseurs Choice, a range of single malts from various districts of Scotland *The distilleries situated in the area of the valley of the River Spey produce some of the finest malt whiskies*

GRAMPIANS

SINGLE SPEYSIDE
MALT SCOTCH WHISKY
DISTILLED AT
CONVALMORE
DISTILLERY
Proprietors: W.P. Lowrie & Co. Ltd
DISTILLED 1969 DISTILLED
SPECIALLY SELECTED, PRODUCED AND BOTTLED BY
70cl GORDON & MACPHAIL 40%vol
ELGIN - SCOTLAND
PRODUCT OF SCOTLAND

History | Founded 2nd June 1893 by the Convalmore-Glenlivet Distillery Company Ltd. Fire broke out on 29th October 1909 and the malt barn, kiln, malt mill, mash house and tun room were destroyed. At its height the flames rose to between 30 and 40 feet. Snow also began to fall, providing a never to be forgotten spectacle. Rebuilt after the fire, experiments then being made with the continuous distillation of malt. Passed to DCL in 1925 and transferred to SMD in 1930. Doubled to four stills in 1964.

Geography | Situated three quarters of a mile north of Dufftown on the A941.

Notes | The distillery accommodated a signals detachment of the 51st (Highland) Division from 1940 to 1942 and then gunners of the 52nd (Lowland) Division until 1944. The distillery is now closed

Water | Springs in the Conval Hills.

Age/Strength | *1969 DISTILLATION 40% abv*
Tasting Notes
Degree of: | Sweetness: ❽ Peatiness: ❺ Availability: ❹
Colour | Very pale straw, almost watery
Nose | Sweet, with the smell of a cornfield after rain in summer
Flavour | Medium-sweet, nutty, spicy
Finish | Spicy, reasonable length
Notes | Gordon & MacPhail bottling

CONVALMORE DISTILLERY

Cragganmore S

Distillery	Cragganmore
Established	1869
Address	Ballindalloch, Banffshire
Map Ref.	NJ 06426
Distillery No.	58

SINGLE *Highland* MALT

SPEYSIDE

CRAGGANMORE

Scotch Whisky

DISTILLERY CRAGGANMORE BALLINDALLOCH

YEARS **12** OLD

SPECIALLY BOTTLED IN SCOTLAND FOR THE
CRAGGANMORE DISTILLERY, BALLINDALLOCH, BANFFSHIRE

History Built by John Smith, formerly the lessee of Glenfarclas. Rebuilt 1902. Extended from two to four stills in 1964.

Geography Cragganmore occupies a site north of the A95 between Grantown-on-Spey and Ballindalloch, close to the river Spey.

Notes Originally only available at the distillery or through independent bottlers, the make is now more readily available. An interesting feature is that the spirit stills have flat tops and L-shaped lye pipes instead of the usual swan necks. The stills have cooling worms rather than condensers. One of the United Distillers *Classic Malts* portfolio.

Water Craggan Burn - a spring on the Craggan More Hill.

Age/Strength *12 YEARS 40% abv*

Tasting Notes

Degree of: Sweetness: **7** Peatiness: **7** Availability: **6**

Colour Straw/gold

Nose Quite dry for a Speyside, nonetheless a richness is present - also quite smoky

Flavour Round, malty, medium-sweet and classy

Finish Long and distinguished, slightly smoky

CRAGGANMORE DISTILLERY

Craigellachie

SPEYSIDE
SINGLE MALT
SCOTCH WHISKY

CRAIGELLACHIE

distillery, founded in 1888, in the *county of
BANFFSHIRE*, stands overlooking the
RIVER SPEY, the rock of Craigellachie, and
TELFORD'S single span iron BRIDGE. The
distillery uses local spring water running from
little CONVAL HILL for mashing, resulting
in this excellent single MALT SCOTCH
WHISKY of light and smoky character.

AGED 14 YEARS

43% vol   70 cl

Distillery	Craigellachie
Established	1891
Address	Craigellachie, Banffshire
Map Ref.	NJ 285452
Distillery No.	39
History	Built by the Craigellachie Distillery Company Ltd, a partnership formed by a group of blenders and merchants. Rebuilt in 1964-65 and doubled to four stills. Now part of United Distillers plc.
Geography	The distillery stands on the spur of a hill, the precipitous Rock of Craigellachie, overlooking the village of Craigellachie from the south.
Notes	Sir Peter Mackie, founder of White Horse, was one of the original owners. The workers in 1923 lived in tied cottages and tended their gardens carefully. The owners of the best kept gardens received prizes annually from the directors.
Water	A spring on the hill of Little Conval.

Age/Strength	*14 YEARS 43% abv*
Tasting Notes	
Degree of:	Sweetness: ❽ Peatiness: ❺ Availability: ❻
Colour	Straw with lemon highlights
Nose	Fresh and cerealy with a touch of greenness, a sherbet character, medium-sweet with good body
Flavour	Fresh, round, smooth, sweet and cereally
Finish	Long and sweet with a touch of spice and a hint of smokiness at the back
Notes	United Distillers bottling

Age/Strength	*15 YEARS 46% abv*
Tasting Notes	
Degree of:	Sweetness: ❼ Peatiness: ❻ Availability: ❹
Colour	Very pale, almost crystal clear watery coloured
Nose	Pungent, peaty, burnt heather with a slight orange tang to the edge
Flavour	Heavy, pungent, peaty, with an edge of sweetness
Finish	Good, spicy, long, reminiscent of Islay
Notes	Wm. Cadenhead bottling

Craigellachie S

Age/Strength	*1974 DISTILLATION 40% abv*
Tasting Notes	
Degree of:	Sweetness: ❼ Peatiness: ❺ Availability: ❹
Colour	Bright straw/amber with gold highlights
Nose	Full, malty, slightly green, medium-dry with slightly smoky oak
Flavour	Smooth, medium-sweet, quite fat and malty
Finish	Long, warm, sweet with a touch of oak on the tail
Notes	Gordon and MacPhail bottling

Dailuaine S

Distillery	Dailuaine
Established	1852
Address	Carron, by Aberlour, Banffshire
Map Ref.	NJ 237410
Distillery No.	46

SPEYSIDE
SINGLE MALT *SCOTCH WHISKY*
DAILUAINE
is the GAELIC for "the green vale". The *distillery* established
in 1852, lies in a hollow by the *CARRON BURN* in *BANFFSHIRE*. This
single Malt Scotch Whisky has a *full bodied fruity* nose and a *smoky* finish.
For more than a *hundred years* all distillery supplies were despatched by
rail. The steam *locomotive* "DAILUAINE NO.1" was in use
from 1939 – 1967 and is preserved on the *STRATHSPEY RAILWAY*.

AGED **16** YEARS
43% vol Distilled & Bottled in SCOTLAND DAILUAINE DISTILLERY, Carron, Aberlour, Banffshire, Scotland 70 cl

History	Said to have been built by a Mr. Mackenzie, was amalgamated with Talisker on Skye and Imperial in 1898 to form Dailuaine-Talisker Distillers Company Ltd. Became part of DCL in 1925 and run by SMD. Rebuilt after a fire in 1917 and again in 1959-60 when increased from four to six stills. Now part of United Distillers plc.
Geography	Situated on an unclassified road between the A95 and the B9102 at Archiestown. It is to the south of the River Spey.
Notes	"Dailuaine" is the Gaelic word meaning "green vale". Situated in a hollow by the Carron Burn. Although electricity reached the Carron area in 1938, it was not introduced to Dailuaine until 1950. For some years from the late 1880s the distillery operated a rail link to the Spey Valley line at Carron station, a few hundred yards away. The steam locomotive which once worked the line is preserved on the Strathspey Railway.
Water	The Bailliemullich Burn.

Age/Strength	*1971 DISTILLATION 40% abv*
Tasting Notes	
Degree of:	Sweetness: ❸ Peatiness: ❻ Availability: ❹
Colour	Straw/amber with lemon/gold highlights
Nose	Quite dry, full and smoky with a rich fruitiness at the back
Flavour	Not quite dry, softly smoky, quite big-bodied, an oaky fullness
Finish	Smooth with good smoky length, but no real pungency
Notes	Wm. Cadenhead bottling

Age/Strength	*23 YEARS 46% abv*
Tasting Notes	
Degree of:	Sweetness: ❹ Peatiness: ❻ Availability: ❹
Colour	Very pale straw, slightly green tinge
Nose	Slightly medicinal, sweet with a gentle smokiness
Flavour	Very sweet, peppery, fruity, spicy
Finish	Fine, smooth, nice sweetness
Notes	Wm. Cadenhead bottling

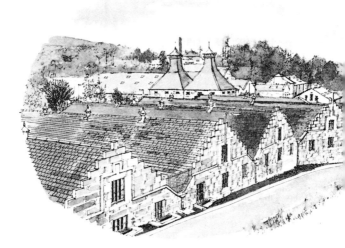

DAILUAINE DISTILLER

Dallas Dhu H

Distillery	Dallas Dhu
Established	1899
Address	Forres, Moray
Map Ref.	NJ 036567

CONNOISSEURS CHOICE

Connoisseurs Choice, a range of single malts from various districts of Scotland.

In the Highlands are situated the greatest number of malt whisky distilleries.

SINGLE HIGHLAND
MALT SCOTCH WHISKY
DISTILLED AT
DALLAS DHU
DISTILLERY
PROPRIETORS: *Benmore Distilleries Ltd.*
DISTILLED **1971** DISTILLED
SPECIALLY SELECTED, PRODUCED AND BOTTLED BY
70cl GORDON & MACPHAIL 40%vol
ELGIN - SCOTLAND
PRODUCT OF SCOTLAND

History | Originally to be called Dallasmore in 1898, the fillings were advertised as Dallas Dhu in November 1899 when it came on stream. The stillhouse was burned down on 9th April 1939. It did not re-open until 1947 but has now closed for good.

Geography | Built in a hollow to the east of an unclassified road which forks south of the A940 on the southern outskirts of Forres.

Notes | The distillery buildings were handed over by Scottish Malt Distillers to the Historic Buildings and Monuments department of the Scottish Office who now run them as a model example of a distillery on the tourist trail. It is still possible to obtain special bottlings from old casks.

Water | The Altyre Burn (known locally as the Scourie Burn).

Age/Strength | *18 YEARS 43% abv*
Tasting Notes
Degree of: | Sweetness: ❻ Peatiness: ❹ Availability: ❷
Colour | Medium-pale, yellowy-gold
Nose | Quite full-bodied, still with a green, unripe character, an oily woodiness and slightly musty apples
Flavour | Medium-bodied, with an oily texture (from the oak) ripe and rich wood
Finish | Slightly spicy, quite long and chewy
Notes | Master of Malt bottling cask no. 1497

Age/Strength | *1974 DISTILLATION 40% abv*
Tasting Notes
Degree of: | Sweetness: ❻ Peatiness: ❹ Availability: ❹
Colour | Straw/amber with yellow/gold highlights
Nose | Quite full, gently peated, oaky vanilla and a slight greenness
Flavour | Round, smooth, medium-sweet with a touch of nuttiness
Finish | Almost dry, oaky with hints of oily hazelnuts on the tail
Notes | Gordon and MacPhail bottling

Age/Strength	*1969 DISTILLATION 40% abv*
Tasting Notes	
Degree of:	Sweetness: ❼ Peatiness: ❹ Availability: ❹
Colour	Peaty/gold, good yellow highlights
Nose	Sweet, oaky, malty
Flavour	Medium-sweet, peppery, good body
Finish	Woody, dry, good vanilla finish
Notes	Gordon & MacPhail bottling

Dalmore H

Distillery	Dalmore
Established	1839
Address	Alness, Ross-shire
Map Ref.	NH 666687
Distillery No.	7
History	Much of the distillery was burned down during U.S. naval use in World War One. Production resumed in 1922. Doubled from four to eight stills in 1966. Two of the stills in use today date from 1874.
Geography	Situated just off the A9, the distillery is in a beautiful position overlooking the Black Isle across Cromarty Firth.
Notes	The distillery was well sited by its founders in the middle of a fine barley growing district. In the First World War, the distillery was used by the U.S. Navy as a base for manufacturing deep sea mines.
Water	The River Alness which flows from Loch of Gildermory.

Age/Strength	*12 YEARS 40% abv*
Tasting Notes	
Degree of:	Sweetness: ❻ Peatiness: ❻ Availability: ❿
Colour	Full deep amber with good gold highlights
Nose	Slightly sweet, lightly oaky with an almost grapey fruitiness
Flavour	Full medium-sweet, quite round and spicy with a slight smokiness
Finish	Lightly malty, smooth and almost dry, quite distinguished
Notes	Whyte & Mackay bottling

Dalmore

Age/Strength	*1939 DISTILLATION 52 YEARS 51.5% abv*
Tasting Notes	
Degree of:	Sweetness: ❻ Peatiness: ❺ Availability: ❶
Colour	Full, rich amber
Nose	Enormous! Soft, gentle, smooth, dark nuttiness, a slight smokiness, very complex with liquorice at the back
Flavour	Very full, quite green flavour - hedgerows
Finish	Long, powerful and very distinguished
Notes	A cask sample from Whyte & Mackay tasted at Christie's

Dalwhinnie H

Distillery	Dalwhinnie
Established	1897
Address	Dalwhinnie, Inverness-shire
Map Ref.	NN 638854
Distillery No.	73

Dalwhinnie
SCOTCH WHISKY
SINGLE HIGHLAND MALT
The Gentle Spirit
An elegant malt whisky with a heathery, lucy finish
YEARS **15** OLD
43% vol *hand-selasan th* 70cl ℮
DISTILLERS GLASGOW AND LONDON

History	Originally called Strathspey, its name was changed to Dalwhinnie when it was sold to Cook and Bernheimer of New York for £1,250 in 1905. Sold to Macdonald Greenlees of Edinburgh in 1919. Acquired by DCL in 1926 and then transferred to SMD. Badly damaged by fire in 1934, re-opening in 1938. Now part of United Distillers plc.
Geography	The distillery is situated at the junction of the A9 (Inverness to the north, Perth to the south) and the A889 to Fort William.
Notes	"Dalwhinnie" derives from the Gaelic word meaning "meeting place". At 1,100 feet above sea level, Dalwhinnie is Scotland's highest distillery. One of United Distillers' *Classic Malts*.
Water	Lochan an Doire-Vaine.
Age/Strength	*15 YEARS 43% abv*
Tasting Notes	
Degree of:	Sweetness: ❼ Peatiness: ❺ Availability: ❶
Colour	Straw/golden, honey-like
Nose	Quite aromatic with a light peatiness and medium-sweet
Flavour	Round, with a honey-like richness
Finish	Good, slightly sweet richness and excellent length

Age/Strength	*8 YEARS 40% abv*
Tasting Notes	
Degree of:	Sweetness: ❼ Peatiness: ❺ Availability: ❾
Colour	Lightish straw/golden
Nose	Light, spirity, aromatic
Flavour	Lightish but round, medium-sweet
Finish	Quite good, spirity

Deanston   H

Distillery	Deanston
Established	1965
Address	Doune, Perthshire
Map Ref.	NN 715017
Distillery No.	86

History	Founded by the Deanston Distillery Company Ltd and sold to Invergordon in 1972. Sold to Burn Stewart in 1990. Four stills. The original mill, designed by Richard Arkwright of Spinning Jenny fame, forms part of an extended complex of buildings.
Geography	Situated on the south bank of the river Teith within two miles of the centre of Doune village.
Notes	Was originally a textile mill dating from 1748, which, like the distillery, also required good water supplies. The River Teith, as well as supplying all the process water, drives generators which provide all the distillery's electrical power needs.
Water	River Teith.

Age/Strength	*12 YEARS 40% abv*
Tasting Notes	
Degree of:	Sweetness: ❼ Peatiness: ❷ Availability: ❺
Colour	Pale straw with lemon highlights
Nose	Medium weight and cerealy with an aroma of chocolate, medium-sweet and fragrant with a mashy character
Flavour	Medium-sweet, good weight, cerealy and smooth
Finish	Quite long and fresh with a touch of honey on the tail

Dufftown S

Distillery	Dufftown
Established	1887
Address	Dufftown, Banffshire
Map Ref.	NJ 323389
Distillery No.	54
History	Converted from a former meal mill.

HIGHLAND
SINGLE MALT *SCOTCH WHISKY*

DUFFTOWN

distillery was established near *Dufftown* at the end of the 19th. The *bright flash* of the KINGFISHER can often be seen over the *DULLAN RIVER*, which flows past the *old stone buildings* of the *distillery* on its way *north* to the *SPEY*. This *single HIGHLAND MALT WHISKY* is typically *SPEYSIDE* in character with a *delicate, fragrant, almost flowery* aroma and taste which *lingers* on the *palate*.

AGED 15 YEARS

43% vol   Distilled & Bottled in SCOTLAND DUFFTOWN DISTILLERY, Dufftown, Keith, Banffshire, Scotland   70 cl

	Purchased by Arthur Bell and Sons in 1933. Originally with two stills, extended to four in 1974 and six in 1979. Now part of United Distillers plc.
Geography	Situated in the Dullan Glen on the outskirts of Dufftown near the 6th century Mortlach parish church.
Notes	From Dufftown which has always been a source of good whisky. It is said that if Rome was built on seven hills, Dufftown was built on seven stills.
Water	Jock's Well, rising in the Conval Hills.

Age/Strength	*10 YEARS 40% abv*
Tasting Notes	
Degree of:	Sweetness: ❽ Peatiness: ❹ Availability: ❼
Colour	Straw/golden
Nose	Light, burnt rubber, floweriness in background
Flavour	Medium-sweet, slightly fruity, smooth
Finish	Lasts well, but rubberiness stays with it

Age/Strength	*15 YEARS 43% abv*
Tasting Notes	
Degree of:	Sweetness: ❽ Peatiness: ❸ Availability: ❹
Colour	Pale amber with lemon/gold highlights
Nose	Medium-bodied, medium-sweet, quite rich and fruity with a slight floral note
Flavour	Medium-sweet and fresh, quite rich and delicately peated with a nice sweetness
Finish	Clean and gently smoky with a nice sweetness

Distillery	Edradour
Established	1825
Address	Pitlochry, Perthshire
Map Ref.	NN 959579
Distillery No.	80

History Founded on land rented from the Duke of Athol, Edradour appears little changed by the passing of time. The distillery has gone through several interesting changes of ownership, the most notable of which was becoming a subsidiary of William Whitely and Company, which it remained for most of the 20th century. It is now owned by Campbell Distillers, a subsidiary of the French company Pernod Ricard, who are investing substantially behind both the development of the distillery and its single malt.

Geography Situated at the roadside at the foot of a steep hill; a collection of ancient farmstead-like buildings, past which tumbles a quick flowing stream. An idyllic setting.

Notes Scotland's smallest distillery whose actual output is only 600 gallons (3,600 bottles) per week. The last remaining of the once numerous Perthshire "farm" distilleries and the last actually distilling by hand. It is run by just three people. The output of the single malt is 2,000 cases a year, the balance being kept as "top dressing" principally for the House of Lords blend. Also known previously as Glenforres, which name is now also given to a vatting of several single malts, of which The Edradour is one. An excellent visitor centre.

Water A spring on Ben Vrackie.

Age/Strength *10 YEARS 40% abv*
Tasting Notes
Degree of: Sweetness: **9**   Peatiness: **3**   Availability: **7**
Colour Richly gold, gloriously viscous
Nose Sweet, almondy aroma with a slight fruitiness
Flavour A smooth, malty taste with a hint of dryness
Finish A buttery aftertaste and creamily smooth

Glen Albyn H

Distillery	Glen Albyn
Established	1846
Address	Inverness
Map Ref.	NH 654459

CONNOISSEURS CHOICE

Connoisseurs Choice; a range of single malts from various districts of Scotland.

In the Highlands are situated the greatest number of malt whisky distilleries.

SINGLE HIGHLAND MALT SCOTCH WHISKY
DISTILLED AT
GLEN ALBYN
DISTILLERY
Proprietors: Mackinlay & Birnie Ltd

DISTILLED **1972** DISTILLED

SPECIALLY SELECTED, PRODUCED AND BOTTLED BY
GORDON & MACPHAIL
ELGIN · SCOTLAND
PRODUCT OF SCOTLAND

70cl   40%vol

History — Founded by the then Provost of Inverness, James Sutherland. Rebuilt in 1884 after being used as a flour mill following a period of disuse. Acquired by DCL in 1972 and transferred to SMD. It had two stills but is now silent for good.

Geography — Sited on the east side of the A9 on the north side of Inverness, it faced Glen Mhor distillery across the Great North Road where it crosses the Caledonian Canal.

Notes — The distillery was closed between 1917 and 1919 and used as a U.S. naval base for the manufacture of mines. For a long time supplies were delivered by sea. Demolished in 1988, along with Glen Mhor, to make way for a supermarket development. Prior to 1745 Inverness had been the chief malting town in Scotland.

Water — Loch Ness.

Age/Strength — *1980 DISTILLATION 12 YEARS 43 % abv*

Tasting Notes

Degree of: Sweetness: ❼ Peatiness: ❷ Availability: ❷

Colour — Very pale straw with lemon highlights

Nose — Light, fresh, fruity and medium-dry

Flavour — Medium-sweet, quite full-bodied and round

Finish — Of good length, fresh with a lingering sweetness

Notes — Master of Malt bottling cask no. 2946

Age/Strength	*1965 DISTILLATION 40 % abv*
Tasting Notes	
Degree of:	Sweetness: **7** Peatiness: **4** Availability: **4**
Colour	Full amber with gold highlights
Nose	Medium-sweet, rich, lanolin and peppery characters with an almost raisiny fruitiness
Flavour	Rich, oaky, medium weight and quite smooth
Finish	Peppery, oaky and dry
Notes	Gordon and MacPhail bottling

Age/Strength	*1963 DISTILLATION 40 % abv*
Tasting Notes	
Degree of:	Sweetness: **7** Peatiness: **4** Availability: **4**
Colour	Peaty/gold, with greenish tinges
Nose	Sweetish, creamy, fruity, hints of almond
Flavour	Sweet, nutty, creamy
Finish	Fine, long and delicately sweet
Notes	Gordon & MacPhail bottling

GLEN ALBYN AND GLEN MHOR DISTILLERIES

Glenallachie

Distillery	Glenallachie
Established	1968
Address	Ruthie, Aberlour, Banffshire
Map Ref.	NJ 264412
Distillery No.	47

GLENALLACHIE
GLENLIVET

12
YEARS OLD
**Pure Highland Malt
Scotch Whisky**

DISTILLED AND BOTTLED IN SCOTLAND
THE GLENALLACHIE DISTILLERY CO. LTD.
LEITH · SCOTLAND

PRODOTTO E ABBOTTIGLIATO DA GLENALLACHIE DISTILLERY CO LTD
NELLE DISTILLERIE DI LEITH SCOZIA
importato da
INC
Ditta Prodruce Bologhi LICENZA U.T.IF. No 18 BOLOGNA

e 40% vol   75 cl

History	Closed in 1987 when sold by Scottish and Newcastle to Invergordon Distillers. It was subsequently sold to the French Pernod Ricard group which also owns Aberlour, Edradour and Bushmills and has since been re-opened. Four stills.
Geography	The distillery nestles at the foot of Ben Rinnes, a short way from the A95.
Notes	A whisky of quality and greatly under-rated. One of the three distilleries designed by Delme Evans, the other two being Jura and Tullibardine.
Water	Springs near Ben Rinnes.

Age/Strength	*12 YEARS 40% abv*
Tasting Notes	
Degree of:	Sweetness: ❼ Peatiness: ❹ Availability: ❺
Colour	Pale, soft golden
Nose	Full and delightfully leafy
Flavour	Full-bodied, lightly peated, slightly sweet
Finish	Elegant and smooth

Age/Strength	*1971 DISTILLATION 18 YEARS 40% abv*
Tasting Notes	
Degree of:	Sweetness: ❽ Peatiness: ❹ Availability: ❶
Colour	Very deep amber, almost mahogany
Nose	Rich, sherried, very oaky, but clean
Flavour	Woody, nutty and quite sweet
Finish	Smooth, nutty and sherried with quite a lot of oaky tannins
Notes	Bottled in 1989 by private individuals

Glenburgie H

Distillery	Glenburgie
Established	1829
Address	Alves, nr. Forres, Morayshire
Map Ref.	NJ 097602
Distillery No.	17

CONNOISSEURS
CHOICE

Connoisseurs Choice, a range of single malts from various districts of Scotland.

The distilleries situated in the area of the valley of the River Spey produce some of the finest malt whiskies.

GRAMPIANS

SINGLE SPEYSIDE
MALT SCOTCH WHISKY
DISTILLED AT
GLENBURGIE
DISTILLERY
PROPRIETORS: Jas. & Geo. Stodart Ltd
DISTILLED 1960 DISTILLED

SPECIALLY SELECTED, PRODUCED AND BOTTLED BY
75cl GORDON & MACPHAIL 40%vol
ELGIN · SCOTLAND
PRODUCT OF SCOTLAND

History | Founded on this site as Kilnflat by William Paul, the grandfather of a celebrated London surgeon of the latter part of the 19th century, Dr. Listen Paul. Silent 1927-35 and acquired by Hiram Walker in 1930. Now part of Allied Lyons and operated by Caledonian Malt Whisky Distillers. Two stills.

Geography | Sited in a valley to the south of the A95 some five miles east of Forres.

Notes | The distillery did once have two short-necked "Lomond" stills which produced a heavier malt known as "Glencraig". One of the main malts associated with Ballantine's blended whisky.

Water | Local springs.

Age/Strength | *1970 DISTILLATION (GLENCRAIG) 40% abv*
Tasting Notes

Degree of: | Sweetness: ❺ Peatiness: ❶ Availability: ❹
Colour | Mid amber with yellow/gold highlights and a tinge of green
Nose | Light, fresh, fruity, medium-sweet with a greenness
Flavour | Light, clean, medium-dry, very lightly peated with a fresh greenness
Finish | Clean and fresh
Notes | Gordon and MacPhail bottling

Age/Strength | *1960 DISTILLATION 40% abv*
Tasting Notes

Degree of: | Sweetness: ❼ Peatiness: ❺ Availability: ❹
Colour | Pale straw, good yellow highlights
Nose | Woody, slightly sweet and floral
Flavour | Medium-sweet, slightly spicy, oaky, quite heavy
Finish | Oaky, reasonable length
Notes | Gordon & MacPhail bottling

Glencadam   **H**

Distillery	Glencadam
Established	1825
Address	Brechin, Angus
Map Ref.	NO 601608
Distillery No.	76

CONNOISSEURS CHOICE

Connoisseurs Choice, a range of single malts from various districts of Scotland.

In the Highlands are situated the greatest number of malt whisky distilleries.

SINGLE HIGHLAND MALT SCOTCH WHISKY

DISTILLED AT

GLENCADAM
DISTILLERY

Trade Mark of Proprietors: The Glencadam Distillery Co. Ltd

DISTILLED **1974** DISTILLED

Specially selected, produced and bottled by and under the responsibility of

70cl   **GORDON & MACPHAIL**   40%vol
REGD. BOTTLER · ELGIN · SCOTLAND
PRODUCT OF SCOTLAND

History	Said to have been founded in 1825, the distillery passed through a number of owners until purchased by Hiram Walker & Sons (Scotland) Ltd in 1954. Now part of Allied Lyons and operated by Caledonian Malt Whisky Distillers. Two stills.
Geography	Situated half a mile to the east of the town of Brechin in the cleft of a hill. Also about half a mile from the River Esk.
Notes	Presently only available through independent bottlers. Some of the make goes into Stewart's Cream of the Barley blended Scotch Whisky.
Water	Springs in the Unthank Hills.

Age/Strength Tasting Notes	*1974 DISTILLATION 40% abv*
Degree of:	Sweetness: **7** Peatiness: **4** Availability: **4**
Colour	Straw/amber with gold/lemon highlights
Nose	Rich, medium-sweet, woody, spirity with a touch of linseed and greenness
Flavour	Medium-bodied, quite rich, soft oak, quite simple and lightly peated
Finish	Light with a touch of spice
Notes	Gordon and MacPhail bottling

Age/Strength Tasting Notes	*21 YEARS 46% abv*
Degree of:	Sweetness: **8** Peatiness: **4** Availability: **4**
Colour	Straw/gold, slight greenish tinges
Nose	Sweet, oily, slight sugar icing nose
Flavour	Medium-sweet, spirity, smooth
Finish	Quite good but with a strong cold aftertaste
Notes	Wm. Cadenhead bottling

Glen Deveron

Distillery	Macduff
Established	1962
Address	Banff, Banffshire
Map Ref.	NJ 694633
Distillery No.	13

History Acquired by William Lawson in 1972, which in turn, in 1980, became part of the General Beverage Corporatio the Luxembourg company which controls Martini and Rossi's world interests. Extended from two to three stills in 1966 and four in 1968.

Geography Situated to the east of Banff on the east bank of the River Deveron, about half a mile from the Moray Firth.

Notes The malt takes its name from the close-by River Deveron rathe than the distillery itself. It can also be obtained as special bottlings as Macduff.

Water The Gelly Burn.

Age/Strength *GLEN DEVERON 12 YEARS 40% abv*
Tasting Notes
Degree of: Sweetness: **7** Peatiness: **5** Availability: **8**
Colour Pale straw with bright golden highlights
Nose Fresh, leafy, quite full
Flavour Medium-sweet, very smooth
Finish Lasts very well, distinguished

Age/Strength *MACDUFF 1975 40% abv*
Tasting Notes
Degree of: Sweetness: **8** Peatiness: **3** Availability: **4**
Colour Quite full amber/straw with gold/yellowy highlights
Nose Fresh, green, leafy, quite full and almost grapey
Flavour Medium-sweet, coffee, very rich, quite full-bodied
Finish Long, lingering with layers of coffee and bitter chocolate
Notes Gordon and MacPhail bottling

Glendronach H

Distillery	Glendronach
Established	1826
Address	Forgue, nr. Huntly, Aberdeenshire
Map Ref.	NJ 624440
Distillery No.	56
History	One of the earliest licensed distilleries in Scotland. Its founder, James Allardes, was a frequent guest of the 5th Duke of Gordon who was largely responsible for the Excise Act in 1823. Purchased by Wm. Teacher and Sons Ltd in 1960. Now part of Allied Lyons and operated by Caledonian Malt Whisky Distillers.
Geography	Situated straddling the Dronach Burn which supplies the cooling water in the valley of Forgue. The distillery is set among tall trees, in which rooks established there, are said to bring luck.
Notes	Built in the form of a square and covering four acres, Glendronach is one of the few distilleries where barley is malted on the premises.
Water	"The Source" - a spring to the east of the distillery about four miles distant.

Age/Strength *12 YEARS 40% abv (Traditional)*

Tasting Notes

Degree of: Sweetness: ❺ Peatiness: ❻ Availability. ❻

Colour Straw with golden highlights

Nose Quite full, medium-sweet, rich, soft, almost honeyed with a slight oily note

Flavour Medium-dry, quite rich, full, smooth with a touch of spice, buttery and delicately smoky

Finish Soft, smooth and long with some smokiness on the tail

Notes Glendronach Traditional is aged in a combination of plain oak and sherry oak casks.

Age/Strength *18 YEARS 43% abv (Sherry Cask)*

Tasting Notes

Degree of: Sweetness: ❻ Peatiness: ❺ Availability: ❹

Colour Deep amber with mahogany highlights

Nose Full, dark oak, nutty, medium-dry with a slight richness

Flavour Big-bodied, smooth, rich, oaky, nutty, medium-dry

Finish Long, dark, oaky with a toasted nutty character

Glendullan

Distillery	Glendullan
Established	1897
Address	Dufftown, Banffshire
Map Ref.	NJ 329404
Distillery No.	50

SPEYSIDE
SINGLE MALT
SCOTCH WHISKY

GLENDULLAN

*distillery, located in a beautiful wooded
valley was ᅥᅥ built in 1897 and is one of seven
established in Dufftown in the 19th.
The River Fiddich flows past the distillery;
originally providing power to drive
machinery, it is now used ᅥᅥ for cooling.
GLENDULLAN is a firm, mellow single MALT
SCOTCH WHISKY with a fruity
bouquet and a smooth lingering finish.*

A G E D **12** Y E A R S

43% vol   GLENDULLAN DISTILLERY   70cl

History	The last distillery to be built at Dufftown just before the turn of the century. Two stills. Rebuilt 1962. A modern distillery addition with six stills was built alongside in 1972. Now part of United Distillers plc.
Geography	Close by the junction of the A941 and A920.
Notes	Process water comes from the River Fiddich.
Water	Springs in the Conval Hills.

Age/Strength	*12 YEARS 43% abv*
Tasting Notes	
Degree of:	Sweetness: **8** Peatiness: **4** Availability: **4**
Colour	Pale straw with a touch of green and lemon/yellow
Nose	Quite full, rich, appley, slightly spirity with a hint of cereals an‹ lightly peated
Flavour	Medium-dry, rich, sweet oaky vanilla, a touch of greenness, spirity and malty
Finish	Long, smooth, oaky with a delicately smoky tail

GLENDULLAN DISTILLER‹

Glen Elgin

Distillery	Glen Elgin
Established	1898
Address	Longmorn, Elgin, Moray
Map Ref.	NJ 237573
Distillery No.	23

WHITE HORSE
GLEN ELGIN
SINGLE HIGHLAND MALT
SCOTCH WHISKY

DISTILLED AND BOTTLED IN SCOTLAND BY
WHITE HORSE DISTILLERS, GLASGOW, SCOTLAND

750ml   GLEN ELGIN DISTILLERY, ELGIN, MORAYSHIRE   43% vol

History Built in 1898-1900 by a partnership of William Simpson and James Carle. Acquired by SMD in 1930. Extended from two to six stills when rebuilt in 1964. Now part of United Distillers plc.

Geography Situated on the main Elgin to Rothes road.

Notes A very compact distillery due to a shortage of capital when it was built. Sixty years were to elapse between the building of Glen Elgin and the next Highland distillery, Tormore distillery on Speyside. An important constituent of the White Horse blend as witnessed by the white horse on the Glen Elgin label.

Water Springs near Millbuies Loch.

Age/Strength *12 YEARS 43% abv*

Tasting Notes

Degree of: Sweetness: **8**   Peatiness: **4**   Availability: **2**

Colour Pale gold with peaty depths

Nose Sweet, slightly green with fine, soft oak and hints of honey

Flavour Soft, pleasantly sweet, smooth, round with honey on the palate

Finish Smooth, fruity and distinguished

GLEN ELGIN DISTILLERY

Glenesk

Distillery	Glenesk
Established	1897
Address	Hillside, by Montrose, Angus
Map Ref.	NJ 718615
Distillery No.	77
History	Closed during the First World War and not re-opened until 1938 when it was re-equipped to produce grain whisky as Montrose Distillery.

GLENESK

YEARS 12 OLD
SINGLE MALT
HIGHLAND SCOTCH WHISKY

Wm Sanderson obon. Ltd.
Distillers, South Queensferry, Scotland
Bottled in Scotland
40% vol   75 cl

Acquired by DCL in 1954 and operated on and off until 1964 when it was transferred to SMD who converted it again to a malt distillery. Renamed Glenesk in 1980.

Geography	Two miles north of Montrose, half a mile west of the A2, south of the river North Esk.
Notes	Established in 1897 on a former flax spinning mill site. Has been called Highland Esk, North Esk, Montrose, Hillside and finally Glenesk. The distillery is now closed again but the maltings are in full production for United Distillers group.
Water	The river North Esk.

Age/Strength	*12 YEARS 40% abv*
Tasting Notes	
Degree of:	Sweetness: **6** Peatiness: **4** Availability: **1**
Colour	Pale straw/yellowish gold
Nose	Spirity, light with a hint of sweetness
Flavour	Quite sweet, full, but with an almost harsh spiritiness
Finish	Dry, reasonable length with a malty end to it

GLENESK DISTILLERY AND MALTINGS

Glenfarclas S

Distillery	Glenfarclas
Established	1836
Address	Ballindalloch, Banffshire
Map Ref.	NJ 212283
Distillery No.	57

History | Founded by Robert Hay, a tenant farmer. Acquired by John Grant who let it to John Smith from 1865-70. Run by the Grant family ever since. Extended from two to four stills in 1960 and to six in 1976.

Geography | South of the A95 almost midway between Grantown-on-Spey and Craigellachie, lying in desolate moorland at the foot of Ben Rinnes.

Notes | Glenfarclas ages very well. "Whisky Tom" Dewar waxed most eloquent of a 30-year old he tasted in 1912 although George Grant considers the 15-year old to be perfection - all a matter of personal taste. Glenfarclas is available at a number of different ages. Excellent reception centre.

Water | Springs on Ben Rinnes.

Age/Strength | *"105" 60% abv*

Tasting Notes

Degree of: Sweetness: ❼ Peatiness: ❻ Availability: ❽

Colour | Deep peaty amber with gold highlights

Nose | Very spirity, slightly astringent, slightly sweet

Flavour | Spirity, malty, a little oily, quite austere

Finish | Long, flavoursome, quite dry

Notes | As the emphasis of Glenfarclas 105 is on its cask strength there is now no age statement on the label. Youngest bottlings are of eight year old with the most recent being almost ten years old (bottled at 60% abv cask strength - 105° proof).

Age/Strength | *10 YEARS 40% abv*

Tasting Notes

Degree of: Sweetness: ❾ Peatiness: ❺ Availability: ❾

Colour | Straw with good gold highlights

Nose | Sweet leafy oak, slight tang of coffee

Flavour | Sweet, smooth, quite rich, malty

Finish | Slightly spicy, long and characterful

Age/Strength	15 YEARS 46% *abv*
Tasting Notes	
Degree of:	Sweetness: **9** Peatiness: **9** Availability: **8**
Colour	Gold/peaty with rich golden highlights
Nose	Full, rich and sweet with a luscious oily character and delicately peated
Flavour	Sweet, rich and creamy, very intense, full bodied and smooth with hints of burnt peat
Finish	Gloriously sweet, gently smoky - long and distinguished

Age/Strength	21 YEARS 43% *abv*
Tasting Notes	
Degree of:	Sweetness: **9** Peatiness: **4** Availability: **7**
Colour	Quite dark amber with rich gold highlights
Nose	Full, rich, sweet, slightly minty, also oak
Flavour	Rich, big, full-bodied, slightly smoky
Finish	Lightly smoky, rich and long lasting

Age/Strength	25 YEARS 43% *abv*
Tasting Notes	
Degree of:	Sweetness: **9** Peatiness: **5** Availability: **7**
Colour	Amber with old gold highlights
Nose	Full, ripe, sweet and round, finely peated with aromas of orange marmalade, honey, coffee and sherry-nuttiness
Flavour	Full-flavoured, smooth, sweet with oaky vanilla tannins and coffee and toffee flavours
Finish	Fresh with a smoky nuttiness and long lasting

GLENFARCLAS DISTILLERY

72

Glenfiddich

Distillery	Glenfiddich
Established	1887
Address	Dufftown, Banffshire
Map Ref.	NJ 323411
Distillery No.	53

History When Alfred Barnard published his *Whisky Distilleries of Scotland* in 1887, the home of the best selling single malt in the world had only just been built. Owned by William Grant and Sons Ltd it today boasts 28 stills, 10 wash and 18 spirit. No mean achievement for a distillery founded with £120 capital and using equipment from the old Cardow distillery; but such has been the success of the family enterprise founded by William Grant of Glenfiddich - the son of a soldier who had served under Wellington.

Geography Situated on the outskirts of Dufftown.

Notes One of only two malt whiskies bottled at the distillery, the other being Springbank. The first distillery in Scotland to open a reception centre, it now attracts well over 100,000 visitors a year. The distillery welcomed its one millionth visitor, Ronald Pedersen, with his wife Peggy, in August 1987.

Water The Robbie Dubh spring.

Age/Strength *NO AGE STATEMENT 40% abv*

Tasting Notes

Degree of: Sweetness: ❽ Peatiness: ❺ Availability: ❿

Colour Straw/gold

Nose Cooked mash, light, soapy, delicately peaty

Flavour Light, sweet, well balanced and gentle

Finish Sweet, medium length

Age/Strength	18 YEARS 43% *abv*
Tasting Notes	
Degree of:	Sweetness: ❽ Peatiness: ❺ Availability: ❹
Colour	Straw with greeny gold highlights
Nose	Rich, medium-sweet, grapey, quite soft, slight tang of coffee
Flavour	Medium-sweet, spicy, slightly peppery, slight green-leafiness
Finish	Good, smooth, long with long hints of coffee

Age/Strength	21 YEARS 43% *abv*
Tasting Notes	
Degree of:	Sweetness: ❺ Peatiness: ❺ Availability: ❹
Colour	Quite pale straw with good yellowy-gold highlights
Nose	Fresh, malty, medium-dry and slightly grapey
Flavour	Soft, warm, grapily fruity, quite big-bodied, spicy and medium sweet
Finish	Herby, long, sweet and smooth with a soft maltiness at the end

AN EARLY CONSIGNMENT OF GLENFIDDICH ON ITS W
FROM THE DISTILLE

Glen Garioch

Distillery	Glen Garioch
Established	1785
Address	Old Meldrum, Aberdeenshire
Map Ref.	NJ 808276
Distillery No.	69

History Established by one Thomas Simpson. In almost two centuries ownership has passed through various hands, including SMD who acquired it in 1943. It was closed by them in 1968 and sold to Stanley P. Morrison who extended it from two to three stills in 1973. Now owned by Morrison Bowmore Distillers.

Geography The distillery is situated in Old Meldrum village, close by the historic Meldrum House.

Notes Garioch is pronounced "Geerie". Waste heat is used to grow tomatoes. The Garioch valley, an 18 mile or so stretch of highly fertile land is known as the granary of Aberdeenshire. Glen Garioch was indeed a canny place to site a distillery.

Water Springs on Percock Hill.

Age/Strength *8 YEARS 43% abv*
Tasting Notes
Degree of: Sweetness: ❹ Peatiness: ❺ Availability: ❺
Colour Straw/pale amber with lemony yellow highlights
Nose Fresh and clean, slightly perfumed, malty and medium-dry
Flavour Medium-dry, perfumed, fresh and quite rich
Finish Spirity youthfulness with a lingering flavour of violets

Age/Strength *10 YEARS 40% abv*
Tasting Notes
Degree of: Sweetness: ❹ Peatiness: ❺ Availability: ❾
Colour Bright gold
Nose Delicately peaty and smoky, flowery
Flavour Peaty, reminiscent of Islay, dry and slightly pungent
Finish Good, smooth, delicate

Age/Strength	12 YEARS 40% abv
Tasting Notes	
Degree of:	Sweetness: ❹ Peatiness: ❺ Availability: ❺
Colour	Mid-amber with good gold/green highlights
Nose	Medium-bodied, delicately peated and floral (almost violets), dry with a slight edge of sweetness
Flavour	Medium-dry, slightly spicy, floral and fresh with good body
Finish	Quite long, spicy and tangy with a green edge

Age/Strength	21 YEARS 43% abv
Tasting Notes	
Degree of:	
Colour	Quite pale with yellowy-green highlights
Nose	Medium-sweet and quite smoky
Flavour	Full-bodied, medium-dry, delicately peaty and quite rich
Finish	Smoky, slightly spicy, quite long with good touches of oak

GLEN GARIOCH DISTILLEI

Glenglassaugh H

Distillery	Glenglassaugh
Established	1875
Address	nr. Portsoy, Banffshire
Map Ref.	NJ 562659
Distillery No.	12

CONNOISSEURS CHOICE

Connoisseurs Choice, a range of single malts from various districts of Scotland

In the Highlands are situated the greatest number of malt whisky distilleries

SINGLE HIGHLAND
MALT SCOTCH WHISKY
DISTILLED AT
GLENGLASSAUGH
Distillery
Proprietors: The Highland Distilleries Ltd.
DISTILLED **1983** DISTILLED
SPECIALLY SELECTED, PRODUCED AND BOTTLED BY
70cl   GORDON & MACPHAIL   40%vol
ELGIN · SCOTLAND
PRODUCT OF SCOTLAND

History	Founded by the Glenglassaugh Distillery Company. Glenglassaugh was silent from 1907 to 1931 and from 1936 until it was extensively rebuilt by Highland Distillers in 1959. Two stills.
Geography	Sited in the Glassaugh Glen to the north of the A98 approximately two miles west of Portsoy on the slope of a steep hill near the sea.
Notes	Very rarely available as a single malt. The distillery was considered to be very advanced for its day when built.
Water	The Glassaugh Spring.

Age/Strength	*1983 DISTILLATION 40% abv*
Tasting Notes	
Degree of:	Sweetness: **5** Peatiness: **4** Availability: **4**
Colour	Mid amber with gold highlights
Nose	Quite full, smoky with an oily-oak character; medium-dry
Flavour	Medium-dry with good richness in the middle, smooth and round with good body
Finish	Long, medium-dry and rich with a nice spiciness
Notes	Gordon and MacPhail bottling

GLENGLASSAUGH DISTILLERY

Glengoyne

PRODUCT OF SCOTLAND

BY APPOINTMENT TO H.M.
QUEEN ELIZABETH THE QUEEN MOTHER

SCOTCH WHISKY DISTILLERS
LANG BROTHERS LIMITED, GLASGOW

GLENGOYNE
SINGLE HIGHLAND MALT
SCOTCH WHISKY

TEN YEARS OLD

DISTILLED MATURED AND BOTTLED BY LANG BROTHERS LIMITED GLENGOYNE SCOTLAND.

70cl ℮ Glengoyne Distillery, Producer of
Superior Malt Whisky Since *1833* 40% vol.

Distillery	Glengoyne
Established	1833
Address	Old Killearn, Dumgoyne, Stirlingshire
Map Ref.	NS 527686
Distillery No.	89
History	Originally known as Burnfoot. Owned by Lang Brothers since 1876, the company becoming part of the Robertson & Baxter group in 1965. Rebuilt in 1966/67 and extended from two to three stills.
Geography	At the foot of Dumgoyne Hill and at the north west end of the Campsie Hills, it has an excellent visitor centre which overlooks a 50 foot high waterfall. The distillery is sited on the Highland line, but, as its waters come from the north of it, it is classified as a Highland malt.
Notes	Although first licensed in 1833, the distillery is believed to be somewhat older. Was triple distilled in Victorian times but now only double distilled. The make is reduced using natural spring water. Not far from the distillery is the hollow tree in which Rob Roy MacGregor, immortalised by Sir Walter Scott, is reputed to have hidden while fleeing from law enforcement officers. The malt used to produce Glengoyne is unpeated.
Water	A burn which falls down Dumgoyne Hill, known locally as the Distillery Burn.

Age/Strength	*10 YEARS 40% abv*
Tasting Notes	
Degree of:	Sweetness: ❺ Peatiness: ❶ Availability: ❿
Colour	Pale straw with lemony gold highlights
Nose	Round, fresh and medium-sweet, quite light and rich with a slight floral note and a touch of greenness at the back
Flavour	Round, smooth and creamy, medium-dry, fresh and clean with good body
Finish	Quite dry with a smooth, buttery vanilla character and a touch of greenness on the tail

Glengoyne

Age/Strength	*12 YEARS 40% abv*
Tasting Notes	
Degree of:	Sweetness: **5** Peatiness: **1** Availability: **8**
Colour	Pale straw with lemony gold highlights
Nose	Medium-bodied, round and fresh, medium-dry with a sweet-oily oak character and hints of buttery toffee
Flavour	Medium-dry, round, smooth and clean, fresh and medium-bodied with a touch of the toffee character
Finish	Long and fresh, buttery smooth and clean with a touch of oak
Notes	Available in "export markets" at 12 years old

Age/Strength	*17 YEARS 43% abv*
Tasting Notes	
Degree of:	Sweetness: **6** Peatiness: **1** Availability: **8**
Colour	Pale peaty with yellowy-golden highlights
Nose	Rich, sweet, oak, light fruit and toffee with an almost liquorice-like character
Flavour	Soft, rich, smooth, with sweet oaky vanilla
Finish	Spicy, malty and nice length, quite chewy

Age/Strength	*VINTAGE 1968 DISTILLATION 25 YEARS 51.1% abv*
Tasting Notes	
Degree of:	Sweetness: **8** Peatiness: **1** Availability: **2**
Colour	Straw with lemon-yellow highlights
Nose	Fresh, slightly floral, medium-sweet and soft with a hint of citrus
Flavour	Very long and quite full-bodied, sweet and slightly spicy
Finish	Very long and spicy, slightly oily vanilla and almost stickily sweet and intensely rich

GLENGOYNE DISTILLERY VISITORS' CENTRE

Glen Grant S

Distillery	Glen Grant
Established	1840
Address	Rothes, Moray
Map Ref.	NJ 276495
Distillery No.	35

History Founded by the brothers James and John Grant who had previously been distillers at nearby Aberlour. Amalgamated with George and J.G. Smith of The Glenlivet in 1953. Owned by The Seagram Company of Canada since 1977. Extended from four to six stills in 1973 and to eight in 1977.

Geography Notes At the northern end of the A941 as it passes through Rothes. The Glen Grant stills are all coal-fired, something of a curiosity nowadays. It is not generally recognised that Glen Grant is the world's second best selling single malt, owing to its dominant position in Italy, where as a 5 year old it has around 70% of the considerable single malt whisky market. It is also Italy's best selling whisky. A supply of overproofed Glen Grant is kept in whisky safe built into the rock in the burn above the distillery. I is reached through an apple orchard. Taste it with water from the stream if you get the chance.

Water Glen Grant Burn.

Age/Strength 5 YEARS 40% *abv*
Tasting Notes
Degree of: Sweetness: ❹   Peatiness: ❹   Availability: ❹
Colour Light gold/copper
Nose Light, somewhat hard and astringent
Flavour Drier than most Speyside malts, spirity, slightly peppery
Finish Reasonable length with a strange heathery tang

Glen Grant

Age/Strength	*12 YEARS 43% abv*
Tasting Notes	
Degree of:	Sweetness: **6** Peatiness: **4** Availability: **6**
Colour	Straw/gold with amber highlights
Nose	Light, sweet, slightly fruity, still astringent
Flavour	Light, medium-sweet, spirity, creamy
Finish	Dry, slightly astringent, lingering

Age/Strength	*15 YEARS 40% abv*
Tasting Notes	
Degree of:	Sweetness: **6** Peatiness: **4** Availability: **5**
Colour	Peaty gold with good highlights
Nose	Sweet, lightish, nutty, slight fruitiness
Flavour	Medium-sweet, nutty, smooth, slightly smoky
Finish	The smokiness comes through on the finish which is smooth and mellow
Notes	Gordon & MacPhail bottling

Age/Strength	*18 YEARS 46% abv*
Tasting Notes	
Degree of:	Sweetness: **5** Peatiness: **4** Availability: **4**
Colour	Full amber with gold highlights
Nose	Full, quite rich, slightly green and a little austere, soft oaky vanilla with a little smokiness at the back and hints of apricots and apples
Flavour	Medium-dry, quite full, round and rich, a touch of toffee and maltiness
Finish	Long and rich with a nice edge of greenness
Notes	Wm. Cadenhead bottling

Age/Strength	*21 YEARS 40% abv*
Tasting Notes	
Degree of:	Sweetness: **5** Peatiness: **4** Availability: **4**
Colour	Amber with good gold highlights
Nose	Fruity, slightly astringent with a note of green wood
Flavour	Medium-sweet, peppery and oaky
Finish	Smooth, well-balanced, dry, of medium length with good oaky vanilla
Notes	Gordon and MacPhail bottling

Glen Keith

Distillery	Glenkeith
Established	1957
Address	Keith, Banffshire
Map Ref.	NJ 427512
Distillery No.	31

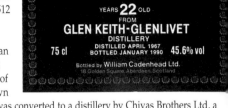

History	Part of an original oatmill of unknown age, it was converted to a distillery by Chivas Brothers Ltd, a subsidiary of The Seagram Company of Canada between 1957 and 1960. Originally designed for triple distillation but converted to double distillation in 1970.
Geography	By the Linn pool near the centre of Keith.
Notes	It was the first distillery in Scotland to have a gas-fired still and the first to use a microprocessor to control the whole operation
Water	The Balloch Hill springs.

Age/Strength | *22 YEARS 46% abv*

Tasting Notes

Degree of:	Sweetness: **7** Peatiness: **3** Availability: **3**
Colour	Bright straw with gold/green highlights
Nose	Quite full, rich, oily, nutty and oaky with a slight citrus note
Flavour	Rich, medium-sweet, gently peated and with an oily creaminess
Finish	Long and sweet with a touch of oaky vanilla
Notes	Wm. Cadenhead bottling

GLEN KEITH DISTILLE

Glenkinchie   L

Distillery	Glenkinchie
Established	1837
Address	Pencaitland, East Lothian
Map Ref.	NT 443668
Distillery No.	99

Glenkinchie
LOWLAND SINGLE MALT
SCOTCH WHISKY
43% vol   DISTILLED AT THE GLENKINCHIE DISTILLERY PENCAITLAND SCOTLAND   70d e

History   The distillery has long been involved in things agricultural, managers in past years having won fatstock prizes at Smithfield and Edinburgh, the beasts flourishing on the distillery by-products. Owned by SMD since 1914 and now licensed to John Haig & Company, part of United Distillers plc.

Geography   Due south of Pencaitland, the distillery is in a hollow in the hills and although the chimney can be seen for some distance, the road end can easily be missed as the sign is traditionally overgrown.

Notes   The distillery has a unique museum of distilling which includes an enormous scale model of a distillery. A part of the United Distillers' *Classic Malts* portfolio.

Water   Reservoirs on the Lammermuir Hills.

Age/Strength   *10 YEARS 40% abv*

Tasting Notes

Degree of: Sweetness: ❷   Peatiness: ❺   Availability: ❿

Colour   Pale straw/golden with yellow highlights

Nose   Dry, pleasantly peated, slightly spirity

Flavour   Dry, malty, quite spicy, full, smooth

Finish   Long, lingering, delicately smoky and quite rich

Age/Strength   *1974 DISTILLATION 40% abv*

Tasting Notes

Degree of: Sweetness: ❷   Peatiness: ❺   Availability: ❹

Colour   Light gold with bright highlights

Nose   Light, fresh and clean, delicately peated

Flavour   Dry with surprising depth and body for a Lowland malt

Finish   Good, long, refined and slightly smoky

Notes   Gordon & MacPhail bottling

The Glenlivet S

Distillery	The Glenlivet
Established	1824
Address	Minmore, Ballindalloch, Banffshire
Map Ref.	NJ 196290
Distillery No.	65
History	George Smith established his distillery in 1824 at Upper Drummin farm, being the first distiller in the Highlands to take out a licence after the passing of the Excise Act of 1823. After the original

distillery had been destroyed by fire a new one was built at Minmore on land obtained from the Duke of Gordon. The very district of Glenlivet is rich in history. It was here that in 1594 the Royal army under the Earl of Huntly defeated the Covenanter forces commanded by the Duke of Argyll. The Glenlivet is now owned by The Seagram Company of Canada.

Geography Notes	Situated on the slopes of the Braes of Glenlivet, the local hills. Though many others have laid claim to the Glenlivet appellation, there is only one distillery which can rightly be called "The Glenlivet" following legal action in the 1880s. So famous had Glenlivet already become by then that the wags of the day called it "the longest glen in Scotland".
Water	Josie's Well.

Age/Strength	*12 YEARS 40% abv*
Tasting Notes	
Degree of:	Sweetness: **8** Peatiness: **4** Availability: **4**
Colour	Straw with a definite greenness to its edge
Nose	Leafy, floral, slightly malty and very fragrant
Flavour	Sherry cask comes through on the palate with The Glenlivet's typical honeyed sweet flavour
Finish	Good length

The Glenlivet

Age/Strength	*15 YEARS 57% abv*
Tasting Notes	
Degree of:	Sweetness: **8** Peatiness: **6** Availability: **10**
Colour	Amber with old gold highlights
Nose	Quite full, sweet, rich and malty
Flavour	Rich, full-bodied and round with a touch of tannin, malty and quite sweet
Finish	Big-bodied, spicy, gently tannic and warm
Notes	Gordon and MacPhail bottling
Age/Strength	*21 YEARS 40% abv*
Tasting Notes	
Degree of:	Sweetness: **8** Peatiness: **4** Availability: **2**
Colour	Full, amber with good, gold highlights
Nose	Sweet and fruity (peaches) with touches of oaky vanilla
Flavour	Smooth, medium-sweet, round and full, gently malty
Finish	Long and toffee-like

GLENLIVET DISTILLERY

Glenlochy

Distillery	Glenlochy
Established	1898
Address	Fort William, Inverness-shire
Map Ref.	NN 113744

CONNOISSEURS CHOICE

Connoisseurs Choice, a range of single malts from various districts of Scotland.

In the Highlands are situated the greatest number of individually widely distilleries.

SINGLE HIGHLAND MALT SCOTCH WHISKY
DISTILLED AT
GLENLOCHY
DISTILLERY
PROPRIETORS D. & J. McCallum Ltd
DISTILLED 1974 DISTILLED
SPECIALLY SELECTED, PREPARED AND BOTTLED BY
75cl GORDON & MACPHAIL 40%vol
ELGIN – SCOTLAND
PRODUCT OF SCOTLAND

History	Glenlochy has always been very up-to-date. Joseph Hobbs of Associated Scottish Distillers sold it in 1940. He established the Great Glen cattle ranch in 1948 which is still in operation. Silent 1919-24 and again 1926-37. Bought by DCL in 1953 when the operation was transferred to SMD. Two stills.
Geography	Situated within Fort William on the north bank of the River Nevis to the north of the A82.
Notes	The old malt kiln has an exceptionally high pitched pagoda roof. The distillery is now closed.
Water	The River Nevis.
Age/Strength	*1974 DISTILLATION 40% abv*
Tasting Notes	
Degree of:	Sweetness: ❼ Peatiness: ❹ Availability: ❷
Colour	Palish amber, copper highlights
Nose	Spirity, sweet, woody, fruity
Flavour	Sweet, woody and creamy, with a note of spice
Finish	Short with a strange woody aftertaste
Notes	Gordon & MacPhail bottling

THE PIER, FORT WILLIAM

Glenlossie **H**

SINGLE MALT *SCOTCH WHISKY*

The three *spirit stills* at the

GLENLOSSIE

distillery have *purifiers* installed between the *lyne arm* and the *condenser*. This has a bearing on the *character* of the *single MALT SCOTCH WHISKY* produced which has a *fresh, grassy* aroma and a *smooth*, lingering flavour. Built in 1876 by *John Duff*, the *distillery* lies four miles *south* of ELGIN in *Morayshire*.

AGED **10** YEARS

43% vol   70 cl

Distillery	Glenlossie
Established	1876
Address	Elgin, Morayshire
Map Ref.	NJ 213572
Distillery No.	21
History	Built in 1876 by John Duff, tenant of the Fife Arms, Lhanbryde. Controlling interest obtained by SMD in 1919. Extended from four to six stills in 1962. The make is important to John Haig's blends, the distillery being licensed to that company. Now part of United Distillers plc.
Geography	Sited at Thornshill on an unclassified road to the west of the A941, two miles south of Elgin.
Notes	A purifier has been installed between the lye arms and the condenser on each side of the three spirit stills. Converted from steam power to electricity as late as 1960.
Water	The Bardon Burn.

Age/Strength	*10 YEARS 43% abv*
Tasting Notes	
Degree of:	Sweetness: ❻ Peatiness: ❸ Availability: ❻
Colour	Quite pale straw with lemony yellow highlights
Nose	Fresh, cereally and green, fragrant with a touch of perfume
Flavour	Fresh with a touch of oaky tannin, quite green and gently smoky, medium-dry with richness in the middle of the palate
Finish	Lasts quite well - clean, fresh and spicy
Notes	United Distillers bottling

Age/Strength	*1969 DISTILLATION 40% abv*
Tasting Notes	
Degree of:	Sweetness: ❼ Peatiness: ❹ Availability: ❺
Colour	Straw/amber with gold highlights
Nose	Medium-bodied, quite rich with a tang of gunpowder and a warm nuttiness
Flavour	Quite rich, medium-bodied, lightly peated with a nice sweet edge and a slightly oily texture
Finish	Reasonable length, rich with a touch of greenness
Notes	Gordon & MacPhail bottling

Age/Strength	*1968 DISTILLATION 40% abv*
Tasting Notes	
Degree of:	Sweetness: ❼ Peatiness: ❹ Availability: ❺
Colour	Palish gold with good bright highlights
Nose	Sweet, fruity, slightly musty, nutty
Flavour	Sweet, fruity, musty, spicy
Finish	Nice fruitiness, good length with a nuttiness on the tail
Notes	Gordon & MacPhail bottling

Glen Mhor H

Distillery	Glen Mhor
Established	1892
Address	Inverness
Map Ref.	NH 654457

57%vol GLEN MHOR 75cl
YEARS 8 OLD
RARE OLD HIGHLAND MALT
Scotch Whisky
GLEN MHOR DISTILLERY   INVERNESS
Bottled & Bottled by
GORDON & MACPHAIL
ELGIN • SCOTLAND

History	Founded by ex-provost John Birnie, Glen Mhor began production on 8th December 1894. It came into DCL in 1972 since when it was operated by Scottish Malt Distillers.
Geography	The distillery was situated at the north end of the Caledonian Canal where it intersects with the Great North Road (the A9) at the north west of Inverness. Across the road from Glen Albyn.
Notes	The name Glen Mhor means "Great Glen". The first distillery in Scotland to introduce mechanical malting, Glen Mhor, like Glen Albyn, is alas no more. Both were bulldozed flat in 1988 to make way for a supermarket.
Water	Loch Ness.

Age/Strength	*8 YEARS 57% abv*
Tasting Notes	
Degree of:	Sweetness: ❹ Peatiness: ❹ Availability: ❹
Colour	Straw/amber, good gold highlights
Nose	Lightly peated with an edge of sweetness
Flavour	Medium-sweet, slightly woody, quite full
Finish	Spicy, creamy, long and almost leafy
Notes	Gordon & MacPhail bottling

Glenmorangie H

Distillery	Glenmorangie
Established	1843
Address	Tain, Ross-shire
Map Ref.	NH 767838
Distillery No.	6

GLENMORANGIE
SINGLE HIGHLAND
MALT SCOTCH WHISKY

ESTABLISHED 1843   PRODUCE OF SCOTLAND

TEN YEARS OLD
The **GLENMORANGIE**
DISTILLERY COY. TAIN, ROSS-SHIRE
BOTTLED IN SCOTLAND

History Converted from the Morangie brewery of McKenzie and Gallie by William Matheson. Rebuilt in 1887 and again in 1979 when it was extended from two to four stills. Owned by Macdonald and Muir, the Leith blenders, since 1918.

Geography Sited on the Dornoch Firth on the A9 between Tain and Edderton, looking across the Firth towards the hills of Sutherland.

Notes One of the smallest of all Highland distilleries. All of the make is used by the owners, none being made available as fillings. A noted feature of the distillery is that the stills have very tall necks, at 16' 10" (5.14 metres), the tallest in the Highlands.

Water Springs in the Tarlogie hills above the distillery.

Age/Strength *10 YEARS 40% abv*
Tasting Notes
Degree of: Sweetness: ❹ Peatiness: ❹ Availability: ❿
Colour Good light gold/pale straw
Nose Slightly heavy, steely, fresh, hints of peat and floral note
Flavour Light, slightly smoky, oily creaminess
Finish Sweet with good length

Age/Strength *1980 DISTILLATION 10 YEARS 57.6% abv*
Tasting Notes
Degree of: Sweetness: ❹ Peatiness: ❹ Availability: ❹
Colour Bright pale amber, yellow-gold highlights
Nose A touch of sweetness, fresh, quite full, dried hay, lanolin and vanilla
Flavour Quite rich, round, medium-dry oaky-vanilla, quite full fat and soft
Finish Fresh, clean, aromatic and quite long
Notes Cask no. 4336; distilled 15.5.80; bottled 5.9.90. Branded as "The Native Ross-shire Glenmorangie"

Age/Strength	*18 YEARS 43% abv*
Tasting Notes	
Degree of:	Sweetness: ❹ Peatiness: ❹ Availability: ❻
Colour	Honey-amber with good gold highlights
Nose	Fresh, salty, nutty (almonds), with an edge of sweetness, quite full and round
Flavour	Smooth, medium-dry, fresh, good nut-oily glycerine, quite full-bodied
Finish	Medium-dry, spicy, long and almost creamy

Age/Strength	*1963 DISTILLATION (BOTTLED 1988) 43% abv*
Tasting Notes	
Degree of:	Sweetness: ❹ Peatiness: ❹ Availability: ❶
Colour	Quite pale peaty/straw with gold and green highlights
Nose	Rich, full malty, oaky with sweet appley fruit
Flavour	Sweet, full spicy, quite green with a toffee-like richness
Finish	Long, spicy, caramelly and fine
Notes	Matured, as all Glenmorangie is, in a bourbon cask for 22 years and "finished off" for the last year in an oloroso sherry cask

THE MEN OF TAIN (Circa. 192.

Glen Moray

Distillery	Glen Moray
Established	1897
Address	Elgin, Moray
Map Ref.	NJ 200624
Distillery No.	14

History	Like its sister distillery, Glenmorangie, a former brewery. Closed in 1910. Passed into the ownership of Macdonald and Muir in 1923. Rebuilt in 1979 when it was converted from two to four stills.
Geography	Situated in a hollow on the bank of the River Lossie, just outside Elgin.
Notes	Close by the distillery is Gallows Hill, as its name implies the scene of public hangings in days long gone. Some of the make goes into Macdonald and Muir's Highland Queen blended whisky.
Water	River Lossie.

Age/Strength	*12 YEARS 40% abv*
Tasting Notes	
Degree of:	Sweetness: ❼ Peatiness: ❸ Availability: ❼
Colour	Pale gold
Nose	Clean, fresh, aromatic, slightly peppery
Flavour	Light, creamy, heathery, medium-sweet
Finish	Delicate, of reasonable length and soft

Age/Strength	*1963 DISTILLATION 27 YEARS 55.1% abv*
Tasting Notes	
Degree of:	Sweetness: ❼ Peatiness: ❸ Availability: ❹
Colour	Rich, mid-dark amber with good gold highlights
Nose	Quite full-bodied, toffee and chocolate, medium-sweet, lightly peated with warm, oaky vanilla
Flavour	Medium-sweet, quite full-bodied, spicy, nutty, almost austere with oaky tannins
Finish	Smooth, medium-dry and quite firm with a smoky touch, lingers well
Notes	Wm. Cadenhead bottling

Glen Ord

Distillery	Ord
Established	1838
Address	Muir of Ord, Ross-shire
Map Ref.	NG 518508
Distillery No.	26

History Founded as the Ord Distillery Company, under which name it traded until 1923 when it was sold to John Dewar and Sons of Perth. Incorporated in the DCL in 1925 and given to the control of SMD in 1930. Extended from two to six stills in 1966 when it was rebuilt. Now part of United Distillers plc.

Geography To the west side of the A832 immediately to the west of Muir of Ord.

Notes The New Statistical Account of Scotland recorded in 1840 that "distilling of aquavitae" was the sole manufacture of the district. Ord - which is built on the site of a smuggler's bothy - is the only distillery remaining in the area.

Water Loch Nan Eun and Loch Nam Bonnach.

Age/Strength *12 YEARS 40% abv*

Tasting Notes

Degree of: Sweetness: ❼ Peatiness: ❺ Availability: ❻

Colour Mid-amber with yellowy-gold highlights and just a tinge of green

Nose Quite fresh and lightly peated with a green fruitiness; medium-dry with a hint of creamy richness

Flavour Medium-dry, quite rich and fresh, full and round with a touch of pepperiness

Finish Long, fresh and quite rich with a dry tail

Notes United Distillers bottling

Age/Strength *ORD 1962 DISTILLATION 27 YEARS 55.4% abv*

Tasting Notes

Degree of: Sweetness: ❼ Peatiness: ❺ Availability: ❹

Colour Amber with good gold highlights

Nose Full, round, medium-sweet, quite mellow with a touch of oily-nuttiness

Flavour Fresh, clean, soft, a touch oaky, quite round and full

Finish Dry, smooth, slightly austere and nutty

Notes Wm. Cadenhead bottling

Glen Rothes S

Distillery	Glenrothes
Established	1878
Address	Rothes, Moray
Map Ref.	NJ 272492
Distillery No.	36

History Built by Wm. Grant and Company. Amalgamated with the Islay Distillery Company to form The Highland Distilleries Ltd. Enlarged in 1963 from four to six stills and by a further two in 1980.

Geography The distillery is situated a short way up the glen formed by the Burn of Rothes which flows from the Mannoch Hills.

Notes The first spirit ran from the stills in 1897 on the night of the Tay bridge rail disaster. The new stills are copies of the older ones.

Water Springs in the hills above the distillery.

Age/Strength *8 YEARS 40% abv*
Tasting Notes
Degree of: Sweetness: ❽ Peatiness: ❸ Availability. ❹
Colour Full mid-amber with gold highlights
Nose Full, quite spirity, rich, dark, lightly peated and medium-sweet
Flavour Medium-sweet, very rich and toffee-like, light to medium peat
Finish Warm, sweet and of good length
Notes Gordon and MacPhail bottling

Age/Strength *16 YEARS 46% abv*
Tasting Notes
Degree of: Sweetness: ❽ Peatiness: ❸ Availability: ❹
Colour Deep gold, quite peaty in colour
Nose Fruity, sweet, slightly oaky
Flavour Full, richly sweet, possibly a little woody
Finish Long, complex, dryish
Notes Wm. Cadenhead bottling

Glen Rothes (Cont.)

Age/Strength	*1975 DISTILLATION 16 YEARS 43% abv*
Tasting Notes	
Degree of:	Sweetness: ❻ Peatiness: ❸ Availability: ❺
Colour	Mid-amber with gold highlights
Nose	Quite fresh, rich and cerealy, medium-dry, an appley fruitiness
Flavour	Medium-dry, fresh, light medium-bodied, rich and clean
Finish	Soft and smooth
Notes	Master of Malt bottling cask no. 10322

Glen Scotia

Distillery	Glen Scotia
Established	1832
Address	Campbeltown, Argyll
Map Ref.	NS 725210
Distillery No.	111

History	The distillery has gone through various changes of ownership, the present owners being Gibson International Ltd. Two stills of classic swan necked design.
Geography	In the centre of the town at the intersection of High Street and Saddell Street.
Notes	One of only two distilleries remaining in Campbeltown (the other is Springbank); somewhat fewer than the 19 which existed at the start of the economic recession of the 1920s and early 30s during which time all were closed. Glen Scotia and Springbank were the only two which re-opened. After £1,000,000 had been spent upgrading the distillery between 1979 and 1982, it was then closed again for several years, re-opening in 1989.
Water	The Crosshill Loch and two wells bored 80 feet down into the rocks below the distillery.

Age/Strength	*8 YEARS 40% abv*
Tasting Notes	
Degree of:	Sweetness: ❽ Peatiness: ❻ Availability: ❺
Colour	Golden with hints of peaty water
Nose	Slightly peaty, complex but delicate
Flavour	Lightish, smoky, richly sweet, slightly spirity
Finish	Soft and long

Glen Spey S

Distillery	Glen Spey
Established	c. 1878
Address	Rothes, Moray
Map Ref.	NJ 275492
Distillery No.	37

History Established by James Stuart and Company. Owned by W. & A. Gilbey since 1887 and now ultimately owned by the Grand Metropolitan Group. Rebuilt in 1970 when it was extended from two to four stills.

Geography The distillery stands just below the ruins of Castle Rothes, the ancient seat of the Leslie family, Earls of Rothes.

Notes James Stuart and Company also once owned Macallan distillery, a short distance away at Craigellachie. Like Knockando, it is an important constituent of the J. & B. blends. The original unit covered an area of 2 acres, the distillery beginning life as an extension to a mill, run by a grain merchant, the James Stuart mentioned above. The maturation warehouse was very innovative for its day, 10,000 square feet covered by two arched corrugated iron spans and supported by decorative iron pillars. Regrettably, on 10th January 1892, there was an exceptionally heavy snowfall and the roof collapsed under the weight of a covering of two feet of snow. James Stuart & Company also owned Macallan distillery, a short distance away at Archiestown.

Water The Doonie Burn.

Age/Strength *8 YEARS 40% abv*
Tasting Notes
Degree of: Sweetness: ❽ Peatiness: ❸ Availability: ❶
Colour Pale straw
Nose Light, floral, spirity
Flavour Strangely fragrant, almost perfumed but velvety smooth
Finish Smooth and slightly sweet

Glentauchers

Distillery	Glentauchers
Established	1898
Address	Mulben, Banffshire
Map Ref.	NJ 373498
Distillery No.	29

History | The foundation stone was laid on 29th May 1897. The original owner was James Buchanan, later Lord Woolavington of Black & White fame. This was his first venture into distilling. Became part of DCL in 1925, the distillery coming under the SMD operational wing in 1930. Rebuilt in 1965-66 when increased from two to six stills.

Geography | On the A95, four miles west of Keith.

Notes | Experiments in the continuous distillation of malt whisky were carried out here around 1910. Closed in May 1983. Sold to Caledonian Malt Whisky Distillers in 1989 and since re-opened

Water | Springs in the local hills.

Age/Strength | *1979 DISTILLATION 40% abv*
Tasting Notes

Degree of: Sweetness: **7** Peatiness: **3** Availability: **4**

Colour | Light amber with gold highlights

Nose | Medium weight with good richness, nutty medium-sweet with an aroma of dried apricots and delicately peated

Flavour | Nutty, oaky, medium-sweet with a touch of spice

Finish | Fresh, smooth and of good length with a nice light nuttiness

Notes | Gordon and MacPhail bottling

GLENTAUCHERS DISTILLER

The Glenturret **H**

Distillery	Glenturret
Established	1775
Address	The Hosh, Crieff, Perthshire
Map Ref.	NN 857233
Distillery No.	84

History Glenturret, previously called Hosh, is the second to take that name. It was renamed Glenturret in 1875, some 20 or so years after the nearby original distillery of that name closed. The distillery, which with two stills is one of the smallest in Scotland, was silent from 1923 - 1959.

Geography Sited on the banks of the River Turret north west of Crieff on a secondary road which leads from the A85 round Crieff to Monzie and Gilmerton.

Notes Now part of Highland Distillers Co. plc, Glenturret is possibly Scotland's oldest distillery. Although the present buildings were erected in 1775, illicit distilling took place at least as early as 1717. The Drummond Arms Hotel at Crieff was the building in which Prince Charles Edward Stuart (Bonnie Prince Charlie) held his stormy council of war on 3rd February 1746. Apart from being possibly the oldest distillery in Scotland (see Littlemill q.v.) Glenturret has another impressive claim to fame in the Guinness Book of Records. A legend even in her lifetime, Towser, the distillery rodent operative, is credited with catching a world record total of 28,899 mice. Born at the distillery on 21st April 1963, Towser died on 20th March 1987, not far short of her 24th birthday. As well as the mice, Towser the cat was also more than a match for rats, baby rabbits and even pheasants.

Water Loch Turret.

Age/Strength *8 YEARS 40% abv*

Tasting Notes

Degree of:	Sweetness: ❻ Peatiness: ❹ Availability: ❻
Colour	Very pale straw with pale yellow-green highlights
Nose	Full, fruity, quite spirity, malty, dryish
Flavour	Light weight, medium-dry, round, smooth, slightly fruity
Finish	Lightly spicy, grapey, medium length

Age/Strength	*10 YEARS 57.1% abv*
Tasting Notes	
Degree of:	Sweetness: ❻ Peatiness: ❹ Availability: ❻
Colour	Very pale straw with pale yellowy-green highlights
Nose	Full, slightly sweet, floral, slightly malty
Flavour	Quite full, round, smooth, creamy, slightly meaty, medium-dr
Finish	Smooth, dry, quite long with soft edges

Age/Strength	*12 YEARS 40% abv*
Tasting Notes	
Degree of:	Sweetness: ❼ Peatiness: ❸ Availability: ❻
Colour	Straw/amber with good greeny-gold highlights
Nose	Rich, sherried, medium-sweet, oaky vanilla
Flavour	Rich, medium-sweet, sweet oak, full, smooth
Finish	Smooth, long, sherried

Age/Strength	*15 YEARS 40% abv*
Tasting Notes	
Degree of:	Sweetness: ❼ Peatiness: ❸ Availability: ❹
Colour	Golden/copper coloured with good yellow highlights
Nose	Big-bodied, full, spicy and medium-sweet with oaky vanilla
Flavour	Full, rich, sweet and slightly peppery with hints of mint and liquorice - very complex
Finish	Smooth, spicy, long and memorable

Age/Strength	*1972 DISTILLATION 40% abv*
Tasting Notes	
Degree of:	Sweetness: ❼ Peatiness: ❸ Availability: ❸
Colour	Pale straw with good greeny-gold highlights
Nose	Rich, vanilla, malty, medium-sweet, delicate oak
Flavour	Rich, soft, round, hints of smokiness, medium-sweet
Finish	Smooth, pleasantly soft and reasonable length

Age/Strength	*21 YEARS 40% abv*
Tasting Notes	
Degree of:	Sweetness: ❼ Peatiness: ❸ Availability: ❹
Colour	Light mid-amber with old gold highlights
Nose	Rich and quite full-bodied, a greenness and liquorice/aniseed medium-sweet
Flavour	Medium-sweet, lightly peated, rich aniseed and creamily smo with a touch of oaky vanilla
Finish	Fresh, clean and long with a touch of sweetness

Glenturret

Age/Strength	*25 YEARS 43% abv*
Tasting Notes	
Degree of:	Sweetness: **8** Peatiness: **3** Availability: **2**
Colour	Straw with yellow gold highlights
Nose	Quite fresh, medium-bodied and medium-sweet; a slight oaky oiliness and a nice citrus character
Flavour	Quite full-bodied and sweet with touches of vanilla and tannin
Finish	Long and sweet, tannic and quite fresh

Age/Strength	*1966 DISTILLATION 40% abv*
Tasting Notes	
Degree of:	Sweetness: **6** Peatiness: **3** Availability: **2**
Colour	Pale to mid-amber with gold highlights
Nose	Rich and quite full-bodied, medium-sweet oaky vanilla with a tang of orange and delicately peated
Flavour	Medium-dry, quite full-bodied, oaky, spicy with characters of liquorice and vanilla, quite round
Finish	Quite long and complex - rich liquorice/aniseed and a tail of oaky tannin

GLENTURRET DISTILLERY

Glenugie

Distillery	Glenugie
Established	1831
Address	Peterhead, Aberdeenshire
Map Ref.	NK 135455

CONNOISSEURS CHOICE

Connoisseurs Choice, a range of single malts from various districts of Scotland.

In the Highlands are situated the greatest number of malt whisky distilleries.

SINGLE HIGHLAND MALT SCOTCH WHISKY
DISTILLED AT
GLENUGIE
DISTILLERY
Trade Mark of Proprietors: Long John Distillers Ltd

DISTILLED **1967** DISTILLED

Specially selected, produced and bottled by and under the responsibility of
70cl   **GORDON & MACPHAIL**   40%vol
REGD. BOTTLER · ELGIN · SCOTLAND
PRODUCT OF SCOTLAND

History | Built by Donald, McLeod and Company. Unlike many distilleries which were originally breweries, Glenugie was converted into one for a while before being turned back to distilling. Became part of Long John International in 1970, which in turn was purchased by Whitbread. Two stills.

Geography | Sited some three miles south of Peterhead, Glenugie is positioned close to the sea, below the A92.

Notes | Closed in 1982. The distillery building, with its cast iron frames, is of unusual and interesting design. Two stills.

Water | Springs in the local hills.

Age/Strength | *1966 DISTILLATION 40% abv*

Tasting Notes

Degree of: | Sweetness: **7**   Peatiness: **4**   Availability: **4**

Colour | Quite full amber with old gold highlights

Nose | Full and rich, quite sweet and delicately peated with a ripe fruitiness

Flavour | Medium-sweet, rich and oaky with a green tang

Finish | Clean and slightly smoky with oaky characters

Notes | Gordon and MacPhail bottling

GLENUGIE DISTILLERY

Glenury-Royal 🄷

Distillery	Glenury-Royal
Established	1825
Address	Stonehaven, Kincardineshire
Map Ref.	NO 871868
Distillery No.	72

GLENURY-ROYAL
Highland Malt
SCOTCH WHISKY
12 YEARS   12 YEARS
50 ML   5 CL
100% SCOTCH WHISKY 100%
DISTILLED AND BOTTLED IN SCOTLAND
JOHN GILLON & COMPANY LTD.
Stonehaven and Glasgow
EST. 1817
PRODUCT OF SCOTLAND
43% ALC/VOL 86 PROOF

History | Originally built as a market for barley in a period of agricultural depression. It was taken over by an American firm, Associated Scottish Distillers and was laid out as a model distillery in 1938. Purchased by the DCL in 1953 and transferred to SMD. Rebuilt in 1966 when it doubled in size to four stills.

Geography | On the north bank of Cowie Water on the northern outskirts of Stonehaven.

Notes | The water supply is also that of Stonehaven. The distillery has been closed for some years, the last whisky leaving the distillery in 1989.

Water | Cowie Water.

Age/Strength | *12 YEARS 40% abv*
Tasting Notes
Degree of: | Sweetness: ❸   Peatiness: ❻   Availability: ❶
Colour | Gold/copper
Nose | Light, spirity, malty dry
Flavour | Light, dry and slightly smoky
Finish | Smoky but quite short

Age/Strength | *14 YEARS 43% abv*
Tasting Notes
Degree of: | Sweetness: ❻   Peatiness: ❸   Availability: ❶
Colour | Very pale straw with pale lemon highlights
Nose | Light and fresh, medium-dry with a touch of richness and appley character
Flavour | Medium-sweet, good body, a slightly green character with good richness
Finish | Lasts well; good, rich and delicate with a dry tail
Notes | Master of Malt bottling cask no. 9776

Highland Park

Distillery	Highland Park
Established	1798
Address	Kirkwall, Orkney
Map Ref.	HY 452095
Distillery No.	1

HIGHLAND PARK
Original
SINGLE MALT WHISKY
ORKNEY ISLANDS
PRODUCT OF SCOTLAND

History	Founded by David Robertson. Enlarged from two to four stills in 1898 when owned by James Grant. Owned by Highland Distilleries since 1935.
Geography	Sited on a hillside overlooking Scapa Flow to the south and Kirkwall to the north.
Notes	The distillery is built on the spot where the legendary 18th century smuggler Magnus Eunson's bothy stood. A local churchman as well as distiller, he apparently kept a stock of whisky under his pulpit. Hearing that his church was about to be searched by the Excisemen, he had the kegs removed to his house where they were shrouded in white cloth. A coffin lid was placed next to the cloth and Eunson and his family knelt in prayer. The whispered word "smallpox" quickly ended any idea of a search by the Excisemen.
Water	From springs below the level of the distillery. The water has to be pumped uphill.

Age/Strength	*12 YEARS 40% abv*
Tasting Notes	
Degree of:	Sweetness: ❷ Peatiness: ❼ Availability: ❿
Colour	Pale straw with pale yellow depths
Nose	Pleasantly peaty with a hint of smokiness
Flavour	Well balanced and almost dry
Finish	Long, distinguished and lightly smoky

HIGHLAND PARK DISTILLER

Imperial

Distillery	Imperial
Established	1897
Address	Carron, Moray
Map Ref.	NJ 222412
Distillery No.	45

40% vol.   *Product of Scotland*   70 cl.

IMPERIAL
TRADEMARK OF PROPRIETORS: ALLIED DISTILLERS LTD

Single Highland Malt

Scotch DISTILLED **1979** *Whisky*

IMPERIAL
Built in *1897*, the year of
*Queen Victoria's Diamond
Jubilee*, the Imperial
Distillery stands
majestically among the
dark woods of *Carron*,
in a fold of the hills
which encompass the
glittering Spey.

Specially selected,
produced and bottled by
and under the
responsibility of
Gordon & Macphail,
Elgin, Scotland.
Regd. Bottler.

History — Built by Thomas Mackenzie in 1897 and transferred to Dailuaine-Talisker Distilleries the following year. It closed in 1899 and was silent until 1919. Became part of the DCL in 1925 when it closed again. Re-opened under the control of SMD when rebuilt in 1955. Doubled to four stills in 1965. Sold to Allied Lyons in May 1989 and operated by Caledonian Malt Whisky Distillers.

Geography — Sited at a hollow on the banks of the Spey at Carron station on an unclassified road between the A95 and B9102, 1 miles south west of Aberlour.

Notes — The distillery is built of red Aberdeen bricks. One of the malt kilns was once surmounted by a large Imperial crown which flashed and glittered in the sunlight. The crown was taken down in 1955. It was one of the distilleries where experimentation on effluent disposal as cattle feed was pioneered.

Water — The Ballintomb Burn.

Age/Strength	*12 YEARS 65% abv*
Tasting Notes	
Degree of:	Sweetness: ❼ Peatiness: ❻ Availability: ❹
Colour	Slightly hazy, pale straw/yellow
Nose	Full, sweetish, malty, spirity
Flavour	Quite sweet, smooth, almost creamy, lightly smoky
Finish	Long, quite spicy, strong and quite scented, chocolatey
Notes	Bottled by James MacArthur & Company Ltd

Age/Strength	*1976 DISTILLATION 16 YEARS 43% abv*
Tasting Notes	
Degree of:	Sweetness: ❸ Peatiness: ❼ Availability: ❶
Colour	Very pale straw with lemon tinges
Nose	Quite full, smoky, aromatic and medium-dry with a green fruitiness
Flavour	Slightly off-dry, smoky and full-bodied
Finish	Long, smoky and smooth
Notes	Master of Malt "Hogmanay Dram 1992" cask no. 7559

Age/Strength	*1970 DISTILLATION 40% abv*
Tasting Notes	
Degree of:	Sweetness: ❻ Peatiness: ❼ Availability: ❹
Colour	Bright amber with good gold highlights
Nose	Medium-peaty, medium-sweet oak, lightly mashy with green fruit at the back
Flavour	Medium-dryish, quite full-bodied, peaty smooth and oily-creamy
Finish	Smooth, quite long, a touch smoky and a peanut flavour
Notes	Gordon and MacPhail bottling

IMPERIAL DISTILLERY

Inchgower **H**

SPEYSIDE
SINGLE MALT
SCOTCH WHISKY

The *Oyster Catcher* is a common sight around the

INCHGOWER

distillery, which stands close to the sea on the mouth of the *RIVER SPEY* near *BUCKIE*. *Inchgower*, established in 1824, produces one of the most distinctive single malt whiskies in *SPEYSIDE*. It is a malt for the discerning drinker ~ a complex aroma precedes a fruity, spicy taste with a hint of salt.

AGED 14 YEARS

43% vol   70cl

Distillery	Inchgower
Established	1871
Address	Buckie, Banffshire
Map Ref.	NJ 427640
Distillery No.	11
History	Built by Alexander Wilson and Company to replace nearby Tochineal. Was owned by Buckie town council from 1936 to 1938 when it was sold to Arthur Bell and Sons for £1,000. Doubled to four stills in 1966. Now part of United Distillers plc.
Geography	Sited on the north side of the A98 between Fochabers and Buckie.
Notes	A farm on the hill above the distillery was once the home of a noted local smuggler by the name of Macpherson. His still, well hidden at the back of the hill, was only discovered when some stray Highland cattle dislodged a large piece of turf, thus exposing the still to the farmer driving the cattle home. Sad to say for Macpherson, the farmer was quick to tip off the Excisemen and claim his reward.
Water	Springs in the Menduff Hills.

Age/Strength Tasting Notes	*12 YEARS 40% abv*
Degree of:	Sweetness: **8** Peatiness: **6** Availability: **6**
Colour	Pale golden/straw
Nose	Slightly sweet, peaty
Flavour	Rich, sweet, full, with a delicate peatiness
Finish	Distinguished, long and delicately sweet
Notes	United Distillers bottling

Age/Strength Tasting Notes	*14 YEARS 43% abv*
Degree of:	Sweetness: **7** Peatiness: **3** Availability: **6**
Colour	Straw with lemon yellow highlights
Nose	Medium-sweet, good richness with vanilla, greenness at back
Flavour	Smooth, creamy vanilla, medium-sweet with a fresh greenness
Finish	Long, clean and fresh with a hint of coffee on the tail
Notes	United Distillers bottling

Inchmurrin

Distillery	Loch Lomond
Established	1965
Address	Alexandria, Dunbartonshire
Map Ref.	NS 394806
Distillery No.	90
History	Built in 1965/66 by the Littlemill Distillery Company Ltd. Now owned by Glen Catrine Bonded Warehouse Ltd. Two stills.
Geography	Alexandria is at the southern end of Loch Lomond on the A82 Glasgow to Fort William Road.
Notes	An earlier distillery of the same name existed at nearby Arroch from about 1814 to 1817.
Water	Loch Lomond.
Age/Strength	*NO AGE STATEMENT 40% abv*
Tasting Notes	
Degree of:	Sweetness: ❹ Peatiness: ❺ Availability: ❹
Colour	Quite pale, good yellow highlights, slightly green
Nose	Malty, spirity, quite dry, slightly rubbery
Flavour	Spicy, quite dry but with a sweet edge, slightly spicy
Finish	The spirit follows through with an almost medicinal finish

WHISKY SLEEPIN

Inverleven L

Distillery	Inverleven
Established	1938
Address	Dumbarton, Dunbartonshire
Map Ref.	NS 398752
Distillery No.	93

History | Built in 1938 by Hiram Walker & Sons, Scotland. Licensed to George Ballantine & Son Ltd. Now part of Allied Lyons and operated by Caledonian Malt Whisky Distillers.

Notes | Two stills for producing malt whisky at the Dumbarton grain distillery complex.

Water | Loch Lomond.

Age/Strength Tasting Notes | *1979 DISTILLATION 40% abv*

Degree of: | Sweetness: ❻ Peatiness: ❶ Availability: ❹
Colour | Mid amber with gold highlights
Nose | Quite light and cerealy with a touch of appley fruit, medium-dry with an edge of richness
Flavour | Medium-sweet with good richness and a smooth, creamy character
Finish | Long, spicy, quite sweet and tangy
Notes | Gordon and MacPhail bottling

Age/Strength Tasting Notes | *LOMOND 30 YEARS*

Degree of: | Sweetness: ❷ Peatiness: ❸ Availability: ❶
Colour | Pale straw/amber with yellowy green highlights
Nose | Quite full, good richness, still with a touch of greenness
Flavour | Full, spirity, dry, but with a richness at the back, the greenness of the aroma is still present
Finish | Long, quite light and spicy
Notes | A cask sample supplied by Whyte and MacKay at a tutored tasting held at Christie's, Glasgow. Lomond is two "Lomond" stills situated within Allied Distillers' complex at Dumbarton

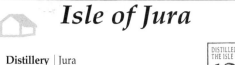

Isle of Jura

Distillery	Jura
Established	1810
Address	Isle of Jura, Argyll
Map Ref.	NR 526671
Distillery No.	104

History   After passing through several different owners in its early years, Jura blossomed in the late 1800s after coming into the hands of Messrs. James Ferguson and Sons in 1875, being rebuilt at a cost of £25,000. However, it closed in the early 1900s because, it is said, of an argument over the rent, after which the distiller upped and went, taking his still and equipment with him. It was abandoned until the late 1950s when a rebuilding programme was begun. The first spirit for more than 50 years flowed again in 1963. Enlarged from two to four stills in 1978. Now owned by Invergordon Distillers Ltd.

Geography   The island is situated north east of Islay. The distillery is on the leeward east coast of Jura, on a bay where a string of islands forms a natural breakwater.

Notes   Records are said to trace illicit distilling on Jura as long ago as 1502. After the distillery had been rebuilt in the 1870s it gained reputation for being one of the most efficient in Scotland. However, it was discovered that the spent wash from the stills was finding its way into a local cattle trough. The effect on the animals, it is said, was most interesting.

Water   Loch A'Bhaile Mhargaidh (Market Loch).

Age/Strength   *10 YEARS 40% abv*

Tasting Notes

Degree of: Sweetness: ❸ Peatiness: ❼ Availability: ❿

Colour   Pale straw with very slight green tinges

Nose   Full, pleasant, dry

Flavour   Very delicate, lightly peated, a pleasant oily/nuttiness

Finish   Very smooth and lingers well

Kinclaith L

Distillery	Kinclaith
Established	1957
Address	Moffat Street, Glasgow
Map Ref.	NS 598640
History	Built 1957/58 within the Strathclyde Grain Distilling complex and dismantled in 1975 to make way for an enlarged Strathclyde.
Geography	In the centre of Glasgow
Water	Local Glasgow water supply - Loch Katrine.

<table>
<tr><td>PRODUCT OF SCOTLAND</td></tr>
<tr><td>CADENHEAD'S</td></tr>
<tr><td>SPECIAL INDIVIDUAL CASK BOTTLING
SINGLE MALT SCOTCH WHISKY</td></tr>
<tr><td>YEARS 24 OLD
FROM
KINCLAITH
DISTILLERY</td></tr>
<tr><td>75 cl   DISTILLED MARCH 1965
BOTTLED DECEMBER 1989   51.4% vol</td></tr>
<tr><td>Bottled by William Cadenhead Ltd.
18 Golden Square, Aberdeen, Scotland</td></tr>
</table>

Age/Strength	*20 YEARS 46% abv*
Tasting Notes	
Degree of:	Sweetness: ❻ Peatiness: ❸ Availability: ❶
Colour	Very pale straw with yellow/green highlights
Nose	Sweet, oaky, rich, full
Flavour	Medium-sweet, creamy, smooth
Finish	Peppery, spicy and dry with a clean tail
Notes	Wm. Cadenhead bottling

*PAINT USED FOR MARKING CASK END ENCRUSTING THE
PAINT POT AND ITS HOLDER*

Knockando

Distillery	Knockando
Established	1898
Address	Knockando, Moray
Map Ref.	NJ 195415
Distillery No.	43

KNOCKANDO
PURE SINGLE MALT
SCOTCH WHISKY
DISTILLED AND BOTTLED IN SCOTLAND BY
JUSTERINI & BROOKS LTD.
St James's Street, London England
70cl ℮ 40% vol.
PRODUCT OF
SCOTLAND

SEASON OF
DISTILLATION
1978
BOTTLED IN 1992

History	Built by Ian Thomson and acquired by W. & A. Gilbey in 1904. Now managed by Justerini & Brooks, a subsidiary of IDV.
Geography	South of the B9102 between Knockando and Archiestown, sited on the banks of the river Spey close to Tamdhu distillery.
Notes	Much of the make is used in the J. & B. blend. An individual feature of the malt is that its bottle states both its year of distillation and date of bottling. If you believe that whisky, like wine, has vintage years then Knockando is worthy of close study. Knockando is "Cnoc-an-Dhu" in Gaelic which means "little black hillock".
Water	Cardnach spring.

Age/Strength	*1974 DISTILLATION 40% abv*
Tasting Notes	
Degree of:	Sweetness: **8** Peatiness: **3** Availability: **9**
Colour	Honey-golden, quite pale
Nose	Lightish, sweet and leafy
Flavour	Typical Speyside sweetness, full, round, good oak
Finish	Long, sweet, distinctive and fine

Age/Strength	*21 YEARS 43% abv*
Tasting Notes	
Degree of:	Sweetness: **7** Peatiness: **3** Availability: **3**
Colour	Straw, light peaty with pale greeny-gold highlights
Nose	Lightly peated, medium-dry, rich and leafy with pleasantly oaky vanilla
Flavour	Medium-weight, slightly green, medium-dry, round
Finish	Smooth, dryish, delicately spicy, quite long
Notes	Known as "Knockando Extra Reserve"

Ladyburn

PURE MALT SCOTCH WHISKY
from
LADYBURN
Distillery
Proprietors: William Grant & Sons Ltd.
Bottled by Wm. Cadenhead, 18 Golden Square, Aberdeen, Scotland
75 cl   46% vol

Distillery	Ladyburn
Established	1966
Address	Girvan, Ayrshire
Map Ref.	NS 398752
Distillery No.	114

History | Opened in 1966 by William Grant & Sons Ltd, but Ladyburn has not produced issue since 1976.

Geography | Ladyburn is part of the complex which includes the Girvan grain distillery.

Notes | William Grant & Sons are also the proud owners of the Speyside malts Glenfiddich and The Balvenie, but Ladyburn is much harder to come by, as it is only occasionally released through independent bottlers, none being available from the owners.

Age/Strength | *20 YEARS 46% abv*

Tasting Notes

Degree of: | Sweetness: ❹   Peatiness: ❹   Availability: ❸

Colour | Pale straw with lemon/gold highlights

Nose | Malty, lightly peated, leafy and slightly rich with an oily character

Flavour | Dryish, smooth, round, soft and peaty, quite simple, but with good body

Finish | Slightly smoky, a touch of spice, with reasonable length

Notes | Wm. Cadenhead bottling

24 INCH DIAMETER QUAICH
(Owned by the Keepers of the Quaich)

Lagavulin

Distillery	Lagavulin
Established	1816
Address	Port Ellen, Islay
Map Ref.	NR 404457
Distillery No.	109

LAGAVULIN
SINGLE ISLAY MALT WHISKY
AGED **16** YEARS
SCOTCH WHISKY

THE STRANGE HORSE OF SUINABHAL – By William Black – "I bet been in Isla more as three times or two-three times myself, and I bet been close to the 'Lagavulin' Distillery, and I know that it is the clear water of the spring that will make the' Lagavulin 'Whisky just as fine as new-milk."

43% vol

White Horse Distillers Glasgow

70 cl ℮

History | Originally two distilleries were set up on the site, the first in 1816 and the second the following year. Lagavulin has long been important to the White Horse blended whisky, becoming part of the DCL in 1927. It was transferred to SMD in 1930. The distillery was rebuilt in 1962 when the stills from Malt Mill Distillery were incorporated. Four stills. Now part of United Distillers plc.

Geography | Occupying a site of six acres, the distillery stands at the head of small bay. The ruins of Dunyveg castle are at the entrance to the distillery.

Notes | Lagganmhouillin - or Lagavulin - means "Mill in the valley". Distilling on the site is thought to date from as early as 1742 when there were ten small bothies there. One of the United Distillers' *Classic Malts* portfolio.

Water | Solan Lochs.

Age/Strength	*16 YEARS 43% abv*
Tasting Notes	
Degree of:	Sweetness: ❸ Peatiness: ❿ Availability: ❿
Colour	Amber with rich gold highlights
Nose	Distinctive, pungent, burnt heather, very peaty and full
Flavour	Big, peaty, dry, very smooth and powerfully complex.
Finish	Long, smoky, almost burnt, very lingering

Age/Strength	*12 YEARS 40% abv*
Tasting Notes	
Degree of:	Sweetness: ❸ Peatiness: ❿ Availability: ❶
Colour	Golden brown like a peat-stained burn
Nose	Big, powerful, burnt mahogany, lots of peat
Flavour	Full, heavy, smokily powerful, strangely sweet edge
Finish	Explosive, spicy and smoky

Laphroaig I

Distillery	Laphroaig
Established	1820
Address	by Port Ellen, Islay
Map Ref.	NR 387452
Distillery No.	110

LAPHROAIG®

SINGLE ISLAY MALT
SCOTCH WHISKY

10
Years Old

The most richly flavoured of
all Scotch whiskies

ESTABLISHED
1815

DISTILLED AND BOTTLED IN SCOTLAND BY

D. JOHNSTON & CO. (LAPHROAIG), LAPHROAIG DISTILLERY, ISLE OF ISLAY.

40% vol   70 cl

History | Said to have been founded by Donald and Alex Johnston. Now part of Allied Distillers and operated by Caledonian Malt Whisky Distillers.

Geography | Situated by a small bay, frequented by otters and swans, it has been greatly influenced by the sea.

Notes | Generally accepted as being the most individually flavoured of all single malts. Although Laphroaig, like all the distilleries on Islay, is built on the coast, it has always been maintained that it is not only the sea air but the peat which accounts for the distinctiveness of the make. The peat, it appears, has a high proportion of moss and this is said to give rise to Laphroaig's particular flavour. For 16 years, during the 1950s and 1960s, Laphroaig had the distinction of being run by a woman distiller - one Miss Bessie Williamson.

Water | The Surnaig Burn.

Age/Strength
Tasting Notes | *10 YEARS 40% abv*

Degree of: | Sweetness: ❷   Peatiness: ❿   Availability: ❿
Colour | Palish amber with slightly greenish tones
Nose | Dry, heavy, peaty and a heathery smokiness
Flavour | Full of character, very peaty, iodine/medicinal
Finish | Lingering and unique

Age/Strength
Tasting Notes | *15 YEARS 43% abv*

Degree of: | Sweetness: ❷   Peatiness: ❿   Availability: ❼
Colour | Amber/peaty with good gold highlights
Nose | Peaty, full, medicinal, slight fruity edge
Flavour | Soft, smoky, round, smooth with a slightly sweet middle to the palate
Finish | Long, smoky and refined

Linkwood

Distillery	Linkwood
Established	1821
Address	Elgin, Morayshire
Map Ref.	NJ 233613
Distillery No.	15
History	The original distillery was pulled down and rebuilt between 1872 and 1873. Became part of SMD in 1933. Rebuilt twice more in 1962 and 1971 when it was extended from two to six stills. Now part of United Distillers plc.
Geography	A very picturesque distillery with a reservoir of water for cooling purposes, inhabited by swans, alongside the buildings.
Notes	Named after a former mansion house which once stood on the site. It is surrounded by woodland, hence its name.
Water	Springs near Milbuies Loch.

SPEYSIDE
SINGLE MALT
SCOTCH WHISKY

LINKWOOD

distillery stands on the *River Lossie*, close to *ELGIN* in *Speyside*. The *distillery* has retained its *traditional atmosphere* since its *establishment* in 1821. Great care ✍ has always been taken to *safeguard* the character of the *whisky* which has remained the same through the years. Linkwood is one of the *FINEST* ✍ *Single Malt Scotch Whiskies* available – *full bodied* with a *hint of sweetness* and a *slightly smoky aroma*.

YEARS **12** OLD

43% vol   Distilled & Bottled in *SCOTLAND*. LINKWOOD DISTILLERY *Elgin, Moray, Scotland.*   70 c

Age/Strength	12 YEARS 40% abv
Tasting Notes	
Degree of:	Sweetness: ❼ Peatiness: ❺ Availability: ❻
Colour	Straw/amber with lemon highlights
Nose	Medium to full-bodied, medium-sweet apple character and a soft smokiness at the back
Flavour	Good weight, medium-sweet, fruity and lightly smoky
Finish	Long and spicy with a nice edge of sweetness
Notes	United Distillers bottling

Age/Strength	15 YEARS 40% abv
Tasting Notes	
Degree of:	Sweetness: ❼ Peatiness: ❺ Availability: ❹
Colour	Quite full mid-amber with a tinge of green and gold highlight
Nose	Quite full-bodied, musty apples and oak with a fresh smokin
Flavour	Medium-sweet, full-bodied, a touch of spice and oaky
Finish	Smooth and appley with a dry, smoky finish
Notes	Gordon and MacPhail bottling

Littlemill

Distillery	Littlemill
Established	1772
Address	Bowling, Dunbartonshire
Map Ref.	NS 442737
istillery No.	94

PRODUCT OF SCOTLAND

LITTLEMILL

Established 1772

SINGLE LOWLAND MALT
SCOTCH WHISKY

DISTILLED AND BOTTLED IN SCOTLAND BY
LITTLEMILL DISTILLERY CO. LTD.
BOWLING, DUNBARTONSHIRE, SCOTLAND

History The distillery has had numerous owners over its at least two centuries of operation, although its origins are somewhat obscure. Littlemill Distillery could be Scotland's oldest distillery. It is possible that whisky was distilled on the site as long ago as the fourteenth century, when the Colquhouns built Dunglass castle to guard the ford across the Clyde. About 1750, George Buchanan, a wealthy maltster in Glasgow bought Littlemill when he purchased the Auchterlonie estate and in 1772 he had to build houses for Excise officers. Annual production in 1821 was recorded as 20,000 gallons. The distillery is now owned by Gibson International, a company formed following a management buy-out from previous owners The Argyll Group. Two stills.

Geography Sited between the main road, the A82 and the river Clyde at the foot of the Kilpatrick Hills, 12 miles from Glasgow towards Dumbarton.

Notes Although strictly speaking a Lowland malt, this is another which takes its water supply from north of the Highland line. Until the 1930s the make was triple distilled. The present stills are of a most unusual design.

Water A spring in the Kilpatrick Hills.

ge/Strength	*8 YEARS 43% abv*
sting Notes	
Degree of:	Sweetness: ❷ Peatiness: ❻ Availability: ❸
Colour	Pale straw with greeny-gold highlights
Nose	Quite light, spirity, fruity, medium-dry, malty, vanilla
Flavour	Soft, spicy, peppery, oatmealy, quite light
Finish	Spicy, reasonable length and dry

Lochside

Distillery	Lochside
Established	1957
Address	Montrose, Angus
Map Ref.	NO 715590
Distillery No.	78

LOCHSIDE MALT Scotch Whisky

Produced and Bottled in Scotland by **Macnab Distilleries Limited.**

Lochside Distillery Montrose Scotland. 40% Vol. Contents 75cl.

Aged 10 Years

History | Established on the site of the 18th century Deuchar's brewery in 1957 by Joseph Hobbs, formerly of Associated Scottish Distillers, as a grain and malt distillery and blending and bottling plant. It was to be run by Hobbs, under the operational company, MacNab Distilleries Ltd. It was sold to Destilerias y Crianza de Whisky S.A. Madrid in November 1973. Originally four pot stills and one Coffey (grain) still, the later was closed in 1970.

Geography | Lochside is at the north end of Montrose, on the coastal Aberdeen to Dundee road.

Notes | All of the make used to be bottled at the distillery by MacNab Distilleries. A small loch once existed opposite the distillery, hence the name Lochside. Most of the malt goes to export, in bulk as well as bottle, with Spain, obviously, being the main market, although some is available in bottle locally. The stills ceased production in the mid-1980s and the plant is about to be closed.

Water | A bore well underneath the distillery.

Age/Strength	*NO AGE STATEMENT 40% abv*
Tasting Notes	
Degree of:	Sweetness: ❸ Peatiness: ❸ Availability: ❷
Colour	Light straw with gold highlights
Nose	Lightish, floral, leafy, slightly sweet
Flavour	Medium-dry, round, spicy, medium weight
Finish	Leafy, hints of coffee, quite smooth

Longmorn S

Distillery	Longmorn
Established	1894
Address	Longmorn, nr. Elgin, Moray
Map Ref.	NJ 234585
Distillery No.	20

History Built by the Longmorn Distillery Company. Amalgamated with The Glenlivet and Glen Grant Distilleries and Hill, Thomson & Co. Ltd to form the Glenlivet Distillers Ltd. Owned by The Seagram Company of Canada since 1977. Extended from four to six stills in 1972 and eight in 1974.

Geography On the A941 Elgin to Rothes and Craigellachie road.

Notes Professor R.J.S. McDowall considered it to be one of the four finest malts. The name Longmorn comes from the Gaelic Lhanmorgund meaning "place of the holy man", the distillery reputedly being built on the site of an ancient chapel. The distillery houses an old steam engine which is occasionally used and also has a disused water wheel. This malt is much favoured by blenders as a "top dressing" for their blends.

Water Local springs.

Age/Strength *15 YEARS 43% abv*

Tasting Notes

Degree of: Sweetness: ❽   Peatiness: ❸   Availability: ❸

Colour Straw, bright gold

Nose Tremendously full, sweet and slightly peppery

Flavour Full-bodied and buttery with a hint of nuttiness

Finish Long, velvety, smooth and very elegant

LONGMORN DISTILLERY

Longrow

Distillery	Springbank
Established	1973
Address	Campbeltown
Map Ref.	NR 718205
Distillery No.	112

Longrow

YEARS 16 OLD

1974
CAMPBELTOWN
SINGLE MALT
SCOTCH WHISKY

Distilled and Bottled in Scotland
J & A Mitchell & Co Ltd
CAMPBELTOWN ARGYLL
SCOTLAND

5cl   46%vol

History	See Springbank
Geography	Longrow is a still within the building which houses and is known as Springbank Distillery
Notes	Although the current brand was only introduced in 1973, the name was established in 1874. The old Longrow distillery is now Springbank's car park.
Water	Crosshill Loch and a spring on the premises.

Age/Strength	*1974 DISTILLATION 46% abv*
Tasting Notes	
Degree of:	Sweetness: ❸ Peatiness: ❻ Availability: ❹
Colour	Pale straw with a green tinge and lemon yellow highlights
Nose	Off-dry and medium weight with a smoky peatiness and a salty/seaweed character
Flavour	Smooth, round, medium-weight with an edge of sweetness and earthy peatiness and a salty tang
Finish	Long and lightly smoky with a nice sweetness on the tail

Age/Strength	*1973 DISTILLATION 43% abv*
Tasting Notes	
Degree of:	Sweetness: ❹ Peatiness: ❼ Availability: ❹
Colour	Pale gold with green edges
Nose	Peaty, quite full with an edge of sweetness
Flavour	Smoky, dry with a touch of sweetness, slightly woody
Finish	Long and round with the smokiness to the end

The Macallan S

Distillery	Macallan
Established	1824
Address	Craigellachie, Moray
Map Ref.	NJ 277444
Distillery No.	41

History Until the bridge at Craigellachie was built by Thomas Telford in 1814, the ford across the Spey at Macallan was one of the few on the river. It was much used by cattle drovers, and whisky distilled at the old farm distillery which preceded the licensed distillery was a popular feature of the river crossing for them. The distillery, although now a public limited company, was until quite recently controlled by the successors of Roderick Kemp who purchased it in 1892. Even today they are still very much involved in the business. The distillery was extended in the early 1950s and again in 1959, but the demand for Macallan fillings has been such that it was doubled from six to twelve stills in 1965, increased to eighteen in 1974 and to twenty one in 1975.

Geography On a hillside overlooking the Spey with the old Easter Elchies farmhouse (it was originally a farm distillery) now magnificently refurbished as corporate offices.

Notes The makers of Macallan have championed the use of sherry casks for maturing whisky and have helped to reverse the trend away from their use. All the Macallan's output is now aged in various types of sherry wood.

Water The Ringorm Burn.

Age/Strength	*10 YEARS 40% abv*
Tasting Notes	
Degree of:	Sweetness: **8** Peatiness: **3** Availability: **10**
Colour	Richly golden
Nose	Delightful, rich and sherried sweet
Flavour	Smooth, sweet, full, rich
Finish	Long and lingering

Age/Strength	*1971 DISTILLATION 18 YEARS 43% abv*
Tasting Notes	
Degree of:	Sweetness: **8** Peatiness: **3** Availability: **4**
Colour	Rich amber with good gold highlights
Nose	Medium-sweet, quite full and with a slight oily nuttiness
Flavour	Medium-dry, nutty, round and medium-bodied
Finish	Clean, fresh, a nice touch of richness and slightly smoky

Age/Strength	*1967 DISTILLATION 18 YEARS 43% abv*
Tasting Notes	
Degree of:	Sweetness: **8** Peatiness: **3** Availability: **4**
Colour	Rich, golden, deeper than the 10 year old
Nose	Rich, sherry sweet, oaky-oily vanilla
Flavour	Sweet, round, rich, velvety smooth, less spirity than the 10 year old
Finish	Long, sweet, very distinguished

Age/Strength	*25 YEARS 43% abv*
Tasting Notes	
Degree of:	Sweetness: **7** Peatiness: **3** Availability: **4**
Colour	Deep oaky amber, lovely gold highlights
Nose	Full, rich, nutty, sherry-sweetness
Flavour	Big, rich, medium sweet, creamy, oaky, velvety- smooth, but woody
Finish	Long, dry, lightly spicy, nutty
Notes	Special and celebratory bottles of Macallan of even greater age can occasionally be obtained

60 YEARS OLD MACALLAN, DISTILLED 1926, BOTTLED 1986

Mannochmore S

SPEYSIDE
SINGLE MALT *SCOTCH WHISKY*

MANNOCHMORE

distillery stands a few miles *south* of Elgin in *Morayshire*. The nearby *Millbuies Woods* are rich in birdlife, including the *Great Spotted* Woodpecker. The *distillery* draws process *water* from the Bardon Burn, which has its *source* in the MANNOCH HILLS, and *cooling water* from the Gedloch Burn and the *Burn of Foths*. Mannochmore *single MALT WHISKY* has a *light, fruity* aroma and a *smooth*, mellow *taste*.

AGED 12 YEARS

43% vol   70 cl

Distilled & Bottled in SCOTLAND. MANNOCHMORE DISTILLERY, Elgin, Moray, Scotland.

Distillery	Mannochmore
Established	1971
Address	by Elgin, Moray
Map Ref.	NJ 213573
Distillery No.	18
History	Built by SMD and licensed to John Haig & Co.

Mannochmore was built on the same 25-acre (10 hectares) site as the older Glenlossie distillery (1876). Mannochmore does not utilise the purifier between the lye arm and the condenser which Glenlossie does. Part of United Distillers plc.

Geography	Sited next to Glenlossie at Thornshill on an unclassified road to the west of the A941, two miles south of Elgin.
Notes	Mothballed in 1985, Mannochmore is now producing once again. Not often available as a single malt.
Water	The Bardon Burn.

Age/Strength *12 YEARS 43% abv*

Tasting Notes

Degree of:	Sweetness: **5** Peatiness: **3** Availability: **4**
Colour	Very pale, almost watery with lemon highlights
Nose	Quite full, cereally and yeasty with green fruit, medium-dry and quite lightly peated
Flavour	Medium-dry, mashy, quite fresh, clean and aromatic
Finish	Light and clean with a hint of coffee, lasts well
Notes	United Distillers bottling

MANNOCHMORE DISTILLERY

Millburn

Distillery	Millburn
Established	1807
Address	Inverness
Map Ref.	NH 679457

CONNOISSEURS
CHOICE

Connoisseurs Choice, a range of single malts from various districts of Scotland.

In the Highlands are situated the greatest number of malt whisky distilleries.

SINGLE HIGHLAND
MALT SCOTCH WHISKY
DISTILLED AT
MILLBURN
DISTILLERY
Proprietors: MacLeay Duff (Distillers) Ltd
DISTILLED 1971 DISTILLED
SPECIALLY SELECTED, PRODUCED AND BOTTLED BY
70cl GORDON & MACPHAIL 40%v
ELGIN · SCOTLAND
PRODUCT OF SCOTLAND

History Said to have been founded by a Mr. Welsh. The earliest recorded reference held by United Distillers dates from 1825, when James Rose and Alex MacDonald were named as the licence holders. Probably used as a corn mill in the mid-1800s. Rebuilt 1876. Was owned by Booth's, the gin distillers, from 1921 to 1937. Taken over by DCL in 1937 and transferred to SMD in 1943. Two stills.

Geography Millburn was located about one mile east of the centre of Inverness, on the banks of the stream from which it took its name.

Notes Fire broke out on 26th April 1922, but the local fire brigade, "greatly assisted" by the Cameron Highlanders, saved the stillhouse and storage warehouses. The commander of the 3rd Battalion, Lt. Col. David Price Haig, had owned the distillery until 1921. Sold for property development in 1988.

Water Loch Duntelchaig.

Age/Strength *1971 DISTILLATION 40% abv*
Tasting Notes
Degree of: Sweetness: **6** Peatiness: **5** Availability: **4**
Colour Mid-amber/straw with gold/yellow highlights
Nose Rich, medium-sweet, delicately peated with touches of oiliness
Flavour Medium-dry, gently smoky, medium to full-bodied, smooth
Finish Soft with a touch of spiciness, quite long and gently smoky

Age/Strength *1966 DISTILLATION 40% abv*
Tasting Notes
Degree of: Sweetness: **6** Peatiness: **6** Availability: **4**
Colour Deep syrupy gold
Nose Woody, slightly spirity, dryish
Flavour Round, slightly woody with a touch of fruit, medium-sweet
Finish A little flat spot, then finishes well, dry finish
Notes Gordon and MacPhail bottlings

Milton Duff H

Distillery	Miltonduff
Established	1824
Address	nr. Elgin
	Moray
Map Ref.	NJ 183602
Distillery No.	16

History The distillery is said to have been founded by Pearey and Bain. It came into the ownership of Hiram Walker in 1936 and is now part of the Allied Lyons group of companies. The distillery was extended in the mid-1890s and was largely rebuilt in 1974-75. Licensed to George Ballantine & Son Ltd and operated by Caledonian Malt Whisky Distillers.

Geography On the west of the B9010 to the south of Elgin. A short distance away across the River Lossie are the ruins of Pluscarden Priory.

Notes In the 18th and early 19th centuries, the waters of the Black Burn supplied scores of small illicit stills in the Glen of Pluscarden, the fertile barley-rich plain being ideal for their situation. Milton Duff is the principal malt associated with Ballantine's Scotch Whisky.

Water Reputedly the Black Burn.

Age/Strength *12 YEARS 40% abv*
Tasting Notes
Degree of: Sweetness: ❾ Peatiness: ❸ Availability: ❺
Colour Straw/golden with greenish edges
Nose Medium to full, fragrant, slightly floral, sweet
Flavour Sweet, fruity, full and round
Finish Almost delicate, refined and long

Age/Strength *MOSSTOWIE 1970 DISTILLATION 40% abv*
Tasting Notes
Degree of: Sweetness: ❼ Peatiness: ❸ Availability: ❶
Colour Mid amber with gold highlights
Nose Medium weight, rich and nutty, medium-sweet with dark oaky vanilla and quite lightly peated
Flavour Medium-sweet and nutty with oaky tannins, spicy, round, smooth
Finish Long, creamy, nutty and spicy.
Notes Gordon and MacPhail bottling. Mosstowie is two Lomond stills within the Miltonduff premises, installed during 1975

Mortlach

Distillery	Mortlach
Established	1823
Address	Dufftown, Banffshire
Map Ref.	NF 328398
Distillery No.	51

SPEYSIDE
SINGLE MALT
SCOTCH WHISKY

MORTLACH

was the first of seven
distilleries in *Dufftown*. In the
(19th *farm animals* kept in
adjoining byres were fed on
barley left over from processing.
Today *water* from springs in
the *CONVAL HILLS* is used to
produce this delightful
smooth, fruity single
MALT SCOTCH WHISKY.

A G E D **16** Y E A R S

Distilled & Bottled in SCOTLAND
MORTLACH DISTILLERY
Dufftown, Keith, Banffshire, Scotland

43% vol   70 cl

History — The first of Dufftown's "seven stills". It was owned for a time by Messrs. J. & J. Grant of Glen Grant and was then unoccupied for some years, the barley granary serving as a free church until one was erected. Extended from three stills to six stills in 1897. Acquired by John Walker & Sons in 1923, by which time it was the largest distillery in the area. Passed to the DCL in 1925 and transferred to SMD to operate in 1930. The old Mortlach was somewhat cramped and was demolished and rebuilt in the early 1960s, re-opening in 1964. Now part of United Distillers plc.

Geography — Sited at the junction of the A941 and B9014 on the eastern outskirts of Dufftown.

Notes — In the hollow in which the distillery lies (Mortlach means bowl shaped valley) was fought the battle, in 1010, at which the Scottish King Malcolm II defeated the Danes. Tradition has it that the distillery is also on the site of an illicit still which drew its water from a spring called Highland John's Well. Unlike most malt distilleries, Mortlach had permission to stay open during the Second World War, except in 1944.

Water — Springs in the Conval Hills.

Age/Strength	*15 YEARS 40% abv*
Tasting Notes	
Degree of:	Sweetness: ❻ Peatiness: ❺ Availability: ❹
Colour	Light to mid-amber with gold highlights
Nose	Medium-sweet, rich-toffeeyed, with fresh peat
Flavour	Medium-dry, rich, quite smoky and nutty
Finish	Quite fresh, tangy, nutty and long
Notes	Gordon and MacPhail bottling

Mortlach

Age/Strength	16 YEARS 43% *abv*
Tasting Notes	
Degree of:	Sweetness: **7** Peatiness: **5** Availability: **6**
Colour	Deep amber with old gold highlights
Nose	Full, deep, dark and nutty, gently peated
Flavour	Full, rich, dark and nutty, big-bodied, smooth and round, soft oaky vanilla
Finish	Long, full, smooth, with a sherry cask nuttiness
Notes	United Distillers bottling

Age/Strength	21 YEARS 40% *abv*
Tasting Notes	
Degree of:	Sweetness: **8** Peatiness: **5** Availability: **4**
Colour	Deep syrupy amber with dark gold highlights
Nose	Quite dry, woody, slightly astringent, fairly pungent
Flavour	Medium-sweet, slightly woody, very smooth and round, full and thick in consistency
Finish	Long and velvety with touches of "sticky" sweetness
Notes	Gordon and MacPhail bottling

Age/Strength	22 YEARS (BOTTLED AT 46% *abv*)
Tasting Notes	
Degree of:	Sweetness: **8** Peatiness: **5** Availability: **4**
Colour	Gold/amber, good yellow highlights
Nose	Sweet, creamy, slightly coconut, oaky
Flavour	Sweet, woody, possibly a little old
Finish	Cold, slightly spicy and oaky
Notes	Wm. Cadenhead bottling

Age/Strength	1942 DISTILLATION 50 YEARS 40% *abv*
Tasting Notes	
Degree of:	Sweetness: **5** Peatiness: **5** Availability: **1**
Colour	Full amber with old gold highlights
Nose	Full, rich and dark, medium-sweet, oaky vanilla with a lightly charred smoky character
Flavour	Full-bodied, round and rich with an edge of dryness, medium-sweet with oaky tannins
Finish	Long, spicy and delicately smoky with firm tannins
Notes	Gordon and MacPhail bottling

North Port

Distillery	North Port
Established	1820
Address	Brechin, Angus
Map Ref.	NO 598607

History It originally traded as Townhead Distillery, changing to Brechin Distillery in 1823 and North Port in 1839. Run by SMD since 1922 and silent 1928-37. The distillery had two stills.

Geography Sited north west of the city centre of Brechin.

Notes The distillery takes its name from the North gate in the ancient city walls, long since vanished. North Port would seem to have been something of a nepotistic society: fathers and sons worked together for long periods and there was little chance of a vacant job unless there was a death. The distillery is now closed.

Water Loch Lee - the town water supply.

Age/Strength *1970 DISTILLATION 40% abv*

Tasting Notes

Degree of: Sweetness: ❼ Peatiness: ❻ Availability: ❹

Colour Gold with yellow highlights

Nose Sweet, heather honey, rich

Flavour Medium-sweet, full, round

Finish Slightly astringent strangely, but lasts well

Notes Gordon & MacPhail bottling

NORTH PORT DISTILLERY

Oban

Distillery	Oban
Established	1794
Address	Stafford Street, Oban, Argyll
Map Ref.	NM 859302
Distillery No.	83

History The distillery was built by the Stevenson family who also founded the town of Oban, which was previously just a small fishing village. Rebuilt c. 1884. Became part of the DCL in 1925 and has been operated by SMD since 1930. The stillhouse was rebuilt 1969-72 and has two stills. Now part of United Distillers plc.

Geography Situated in the centre and built before most of the town.

Notes Nose and flavour are reminiscent of Bowmore although more subtle and delicate. One of the United Distillers' *Classic Malts* portfolio.

Water Two lochs in Ardconnel, one mile above the town.

Age/Strength *14 YEARS 43% abv*

Tasting Notes

Degree of: Sweetness: ❺ Peatiness: ❼ Availability: ❻

Colour Very pale straw with gold highlights

Nose Medium-sweet, lightly peated, quite rich, slight burnt heather

Flavour Smooth, lightly sweet, creamy, very delicate peatiness

Finish Smoky, dry and delicate

OBAN DISTILLERY

Old Fettercairn

Distillery	Fettercairn
Established	1824
Address	Fettercairn, Kincardine
Map Ref.	NO 645737
Distillery No.	75

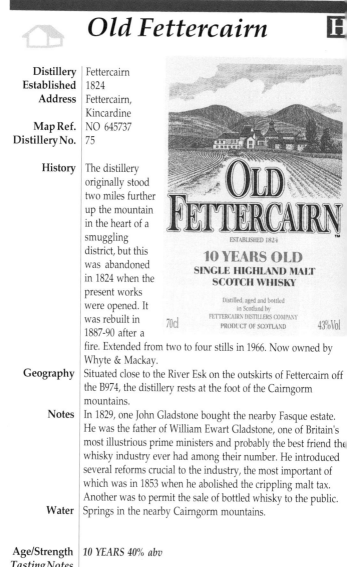

OLD FETTERCAIRN

ESTABLISHED 1824

10 YEARS OLD
SINGLE HIGHLAND MALT
SCOTCH WHISKY

Distilled, aged and bottled
in Scotland by
FETTERCAIRN DISTILLERS COMPANY
PRODUCT OF SCOTLAND

70cl   43%Vol

History	The distillery originally stood two miles further up the mountain in the heart of a smuggling district, but this was abandoned in 1824 when the present works were opened. It was rebuilt in 1887-90 after a fire. Extended from two to four stills in 1966. Now owned by Whyte & Mackay.
Geography	Situated close to the River Esk on the outskirts of Fettercairn off the B974, the distillery rests at the foot of the Cairngorm mountains.
Notes	In 1829, one John Gladstone bought the nearby Fasque estate. He was the father of William Ewart Gladstone, one of Britain's most illustrious prime ministers and probably the best friend the whisky industry ever had among their number. He introduced several reforms crucial to the industry, the most important of which was in 1853 when he abolished the crippling malt tax. Another was to permit the sale of bottled whisky to the public.
Water	Springs in the nearby Cairngorm mountains.

Age/Strength	*10 YEARS 40% abv*
Tasting Notes	
Degree of:	Sweetness: ❹ Peatiness: ❹ Availability: ❺
Colour	Straw with good gold highlights
Nose	Quite full, dryish, vanilla oak, malty
Flavour	Dry, spicy, medium weight, creamy smooth
Finish	Dry, long and chewy

Old Pulteney

Distillery	Pulteney
Established	1826
Address	Wick, Caithness
Map Ref.	ND 368501
Distillery No.	3

History Established by one James Henderson. Became part of the DCL in 1925, having been purchased by John Dewar & Sons a couple of years earlier. Closed between 1930 and 1951, then revived. In 1955 it was bought by Hiram Walker, now part of Allied Lyons, who rebuilt the distillery in 1959. Has two stills and is operated by Caledonian Malt Whisky Distillers.

Geography The most northerly distillery on the U.K. mainland. It is sited on the southern side of Wick, close to the North Sea coast.

Notes Only available from the independent bottlers, in this case, Gordon & MacPhail. It is reputed to be one of the fastest maturing of malt whiskies. One of the main malts associated with Ballantine's blended Scotch Whisky.

Water The Loch of Hempriggs.

Age/Strength *8 YEARS 40% abv*

Tasting Notes

Degree of: Sweetness: ❸ Peatiness: ❽ Availability: ❹

Colour Palish gold with tinges of green

Nose Delicately pungent, faint tangs of ozone

Flavour Quite pungent, smoky, clean

Finish Smoky, dry, refreshing

OLD PULTENEY DISTILLERY

Pittyvaich

Distillery	Pittyvaich
Established	1975
Address	Dufftown, Banffshire
Map Ref.	NJ 323390
Distillery No.	55
History	Built by Arthur Bell & Sons Ltd as a sister to Dufftown and operated in conjunction with it. Four stills. Now part of United Distillers plc.
Geography	Situated in the Dullan Glen on the outskirts of Dufftown near the 6th century Mortlach parish church.
Notes	The make uses the same water source as Dufftown and gives a similar whisky.
Water	The distillery draws its mashing water from two springs, Convalleys and Balliemore.

SPEYSIDE
SINGLE MALT
SCOTCH WHISKY

PITTYVAICH

distillery is situated in the DULLAN GLEN on the outskirts of Dufftown, near to the historic Mortlach Church which dates back to the 6th. The distillery draws water from two nearby springs - CONVALLEYS and BALLIEMORE. Pittyvaich single MALT SCOTCH WHISKY has a perfumed, fruity nose and a robust flavour with a hint of spiciness.

AGED **12** YEARS

Distilled & Bonded in SCOTLAND
PITTYVAICH DISTILLERY
Dufftown, Keith, Banffshire, Scotland
43% vol   70 cl

Age/Strength	*12 YEARS 43% abv*
Tasting Notes	
Degree of:	Sweetness: ❹ Peatiness: ❻ Availability: ❻
Colour	Amber with old gold highlights
Nose	Round, quite full, malty, spicy, peppery and almost meaty with coffee at the back
Flavour	Medium-dry, quite full-bodied and dark flavoured with a touc of tannin
Finish	Long-chewy and quite big
Notes	United Distillers bottling

Age/Strength	*12 YEARS 54% abv*
Tasting Notes	
Degree of:	Sweetness: ❺ Peatiness: ❼ Availability: ❸
Colour	Medium-pale amber with lemony highlights
Nose	Medium-bodied, spirity, a hint of toffee/coffee, greenness at back
Flavour	Medium-dry, coffee, quite full, round and smooth
Finish	Creamy, quite sweet, tangy and long, with a touch of smokines on the tail
Notes	James MacArthur bottling cask no. 15096

Pittyvaich

Age/Strength	*12 YEARS 56.6% abv*
Tasting Notes	
Degree of:	Sweetness: ❹ Peatiness: ❼ Availability: ❹
Colour	Straw/amber with pale gold highlights
Nose	Quite peaty, soft, damp oak with a touch of green, unripe coffee
Flavour	Medium-dry, coffee/chocolate, smoky peatiness with a touch of spice
Finish	Long, lingering, spicy, smooth and nutty
Notes	Wm. Cadenhead bottling

Age/Strength	*13 YEARS 58% abv*
Tasting Notes	
Degree of:	Sweetness: ❹ Peatiness: ❼ Availability: ❹
Colour	Deep cough linctus amber with bronze highlights
Nose	Big-bodied, dark, rich, malty cerealy, touch of rubber
Flavour	Big, dark, rich, cerealy and smoky with a little spice
Finish	Quite spirity, long and smoky with a rich centre
Notes	Wm. Cadenhead bottling

POT STILLS

131

Port Ellen

Distillery	Port Ellen
Established	1825
Address	Port Ellen, Islay
Map Ref.	NR 358458

CONNOISSEURS CHOICE

Connoisseurs Choice, a range of single malts from various districts of Scotland.

The island of Islay traditionally produces heavy peated and smoky whiskies.

SINGLE ISLAY MALT SCOTCH WHISKY
DISTILLED AT
PORT ELLEN
DISTILLERY
PROPRIETORS: Low Robertson & Co. Ltd
DISTILLED **1977** DISTILLED

SPECIALLY SELECTED, PRODUCED AND BOTTLED BY
70cl **GORDON & MACPHAIL** 40%vol
ELGIN · SCOTLAND
PRODUCT OF SCOTLAND

History | Founded by A.K. Mackay & Company. Acquired by John Ramsay and run by him and his heirs until 1920. Bought by the DCL in 1927 and transferred to SMD in 1930. Silent 1929 to 1966, although the maltings continued in use. The distillery was extensively rebuilt in 1967 when increased from two to four stills. A large new maltings was erected in 1973. Although the distillery ceased production again in May 1983, the maltings now serves all the Islay distilleries following an historic agreement between the producing companies in 1987.

Geography | Situated about half a mile from Port Ellen, the maltings building now dominates the shoreline.

Notes | The Excise Act of 1824 enforced the introduction of the spirit safe in distilleries. Tests had to be made to ensure that it had no harmful effects on the make. The official experiments were carried out in Port Ellen. The maltings were visited by Her Majesty Queen Elizabeth II on 11th August 1980.

Water | Two local lochs.

Age/Strength	*13 YEARS 43% abv*
Tasting Notes	
Degree of:	Sweetness: ❸ Peatiness: ❾ Availability: ❷
Colour	Very pale, almost exceptionally so, hints of lemony/yellow
Nose	Medium to full-bodied, a burnt, peat character and a greenness at the back with a rich lanolin-oily character
Flavour	Smoky, quite rich, pungent and full with good sweet oak
Finish	Long and smooth with smoky oaky vanilla
Notes	Master of Malt bottling cask nos. 1832 - 1836

Port Ellen

Age/Strength Tasting Notes	*1971 DISTILLATION 40% abv*
Degree of:	Sweetness: ❷ Peatiness: ❾ Availability: ❹
Colour	Bright gold/amber with good yellow highlights
Nose	Smoky peat, ozone, burnt heather roots with a very slight hint of sweetness
Flavour	Quite full, round, smoky, quite smooth and almost medicinal
Finish	Smoky with the burnt heather roots lingering
Notes	Gordon and MacPhail bottling
Age/Strength Tasting Notes	*1970 DISTILLATION 40% abv*
Degree of:	Sweetness: ❷ Peatiness: ❾ Availability: ❹
Colour	Peaty/gold with bright highlights
Nose	Big, pungent, peaty, slightly rubbery, dry
Flavour	Big, burnt peat, an edge of sweetness, very distinctive
Finish	Long, pungent and smoky
Notes	Gordon and MacPhail bottling

PORT ELLEN DISTILLERY AND MALTINGS

Rosebank

Distillery	Rosebank
Established	1840
Address	Falkirk, Stirlingshire
Map Ref.	NS 876803

History The distillery, established by James Rankine, is said to have been converted from the maltings of the earlier Camelon distillery. Rebuilt in 1864. In 1914 the Rosebank Distillery Ltd, as it was then called, was one of the companies merged into the formation of Scottish Malt Distillers Ltd. Now part of United Distillers plc.

LOWLAND
SINGLE MALT
SCOTCH WHISKY

Established on its present site at *CAMELON* in 1840

ROSEBANK

distillery stands on the banks of the *FORTH* and *CLYDE CANAL*. This was once a busy thoroughfare with boats and steamers continually passing by; it is still the source of water for cooling. This single *MALT SCOTCH WHISKY* is *triple distilled* which accounts for its *light distinctive nose* and *well balanced* flavour.

A G E D **12** Y E A R S

Distilled & Bottled in *SCOTLAND*.
ROSEBANK DISTILLERY
Falkirk, Stirlingshire, Scotland.
43% vol   70 cl

Geography Sited on the banks of the Forth and Clyde canal where the A80 intersects with the canal on the north side of Falkirk.

Notes The make is triple distilled. Distillery closed May 1993.

Water Carron Valley Reservoir.

Age/Strength	*12 YEARS 43% abv*
Tasting Notes	
Degree of:	Sweetness: ❷ Peatiness: ❹ Availability: ❹
Colour	Straw/light amber with gold and lemon highlights
Nose	Medium-bodied, spirity with a touch of greenness, lightly oily
Flavour	Light, smooth, dryish with mashy characters
Finish	Smooth, dry, oaky with pleasant lightness
Notes	United Distillers bottling

Age/Strength	*17 YEARS 43% abv*
Tasting Notes	
Degree of:	Sweetness: ❷ Peatiness: ❹ Availability: ❶
Colour	Mid-amber/yellow with a touch of green
Nose	Medium-bodied, dryish, but with a richness at the back, a green nuttiness, malty with an almost honeyed touch
Flavour	Dry, spicy, quite full-bodied, round, soft and smooth
Finish	Long and quite rich with a toffee-like tail
Notes	Master of Malt bottling - cask no. 5064

Royal Brackla   H

Distillery	Royal Brackla
Established	1812
Address	Nairn
Map Ref.	NH 862515

HIGHLAND
SINGLE MALT SCOTCH WHISKY
ROYAL BRACKLA
distillery, established in 1812, lies on the
southern shore of the *MORAY FIRTH* at *Cawdor* near *Nairn*.
Woods around the *distillery* are home to the *SISKIN*;
although a *shy bird*, it can often be seen *feeding* on conifer seeds.

In 1835 a *Royal Warrant* was granted to the *distillery* by King William IV,
who enjoyed the *fresh, grassy, fruity* aroma of this *single malt whisky*.

43% vol   A G E D **10** Y E A R S   70 cl
Distilled & Bottled in SCOTLAND. ROYAL BRACKLA DISTILLERY, Cawdor, Nairn, Scotland

History Said to have been founded by Captain William Fraser. Purchased by SMD in 1943. Rebuilt 1965-66 and extended from two to four stills in 1970.

Geography Sited to the north west of the B9090, one mile south of Nairn.

Notes Brackla was the first distillery to be granted a Royal warrant in 1835. It was referred to at that time as "Brackla" or "The King's own Whisky". Some of the older buildings were converted to a visitor centre in 1982/83, it being three quarters of a mile from Cawdor Castle, but regrettably, the distillery was closed in May 1993.

Water The Cawdor Burn.

Age/Strength *10 YEARS 43% abv*
Tasting Notes
Degree of: Sweetness: ❼ Peatiness: ❺ Availability: ❻
Colour Quite pale straw with yellow highlights
Nose Fresh, clean and medium-sweet with a fruitiness and a floral note, gentle peat in the background
Flavour Round, medium-sweet and quite full-bodied with a green fruity character
Finish Long, fresh and clean
Notes United Distillers bottling

Age/Strength *18 YEARS 46% abv*
Tasting Notes
Degree of: Sweetness: ❽ Peatiness: ❺ Availability: ❹
Colour Pale straw, good yellow highlights, definite green tinge
Nose Round, sweet and fruity
Flavour Sweet, smooth, round, rich
Finish Velvety smooth, long and distinguished
Notes Wm. Cadenhead bottling

Royal Brackla (Cont.)

Age/Strength	*1970 DISTILLATION 40% abv*
Tasting Notes	
Degree of:	Sweetness: ❼ Peatiness: ❻ Availability: ❹
Colour	Pale-mid amber with yellow gold highlights
Nose	Good body with oak, cold apples and a peaty smokiness
Flavour	Medium-dry, oaky, quite mellow and smooth with a slight oiliness and medium peatiness
Finish	Reasonable oaky finish with a touch of richness
Notes	Gordon and MacPhail bottling

ROYAL BRACKLA DISTILLERY

Royal Lochnagar H

Distillery	Royal Lochnagar
Established	1845
Address	Crathie, Ballater, Aberdeenshire
Map Ref.	NO 267938
Distillery No.	71

History | Originally known as "New Lochnagar", as another Lochnagar distillery had been built nearby in 1826. It obtained the Royal warrant after its owner, John Begg, had invited Queen Victoria and Prince Albert to view the distillery in 1848. The buildings were rebuilt in 1906. Two stills. Now part of United Distillers plc.

Geography | The only remaining distillery on Deeside. It overlooks Balmoral Castle.

Notes | Close to the royal residence of Balmoral, Royal Lochnagar has a very popular visitor centre, converted in 1987 from old distillery buildings.

Water | Springs in the foothills of Lochnagar.

Age/Strength | *12 YEARS 40% abv*
Tasting Notes
Degree of: | Sweetness: ❽ Peatiness: ❹ Availability: ❺
Colour | Pale straw, bright gold highlights
Nose | Pleasant, slightly peppery and fruity
Flavour | Sweet, clean, creamy, slightly peppery
Finish | Good smooth length

Age/Strength | *SELECTED RESERVE 43% abv*
Tasting Notes
Degree of: | Sweetness: ❽ Peatiness: ❸ Availability: ❸
Colour | Deep peaty amber with good gold highlights
Nose | Rich, wet oak, vanilla, sweet, lightly sherried
Flavour | Full, round, rich and mellow, nutty and creamy
Finish | Long, slightly spicy and very smooth

St. Magdalene L

Distillery	St. Magdalene
Established	c. 1795
Address	Linlithgow, West Lothian
Map Ref.	NT 008771

> CONNOISSEURS CHOICE
>
> *Connoisseurs Choice: a range of single malts from various districts of Scotland.*
>
> *The lowlands traditionally produce smooth soft and mellow whiskies.*
>
> SINGLE LOWLAND MALT SCOTCH WHISKY
> **ST. MAGDALENE**
> DISTILLERY
> *Proprietors: John Napier & Co. Ltd*
> DISTILLED **1965** DISTILLED
> SPECIALLY SELECTED, PRODUCED AND BOTTLED BY
> **GORDON & MACPHAIL**
> ELGIN · SCOTLAND
> PRODUCT OF SCOTLAND
> 70cl   40%vol

History Said to have been founded by Sebastian Henderson in the 18th century at St. Magdalene's Cross. The former site of an annual fair and of St. Magdalene's Hospital, St. Magdalene was one of five distilleries which formed Scottish Malt Distillers in July 1914.

Geography Sited at the eastern end of Linlithgow where the railway line, running alongside the Union Canal, intersects with the A706.

Notes Linlithgow was a centre of milling and malting in the 17th century and of brewing and distilling in the 18th century. The distillery is now closed and part has been developed for housing.

Water The town's domestic supply, which comes from Loch Lomond.

Age/Strength *1965 DISTILLATION 40% abv*
Tasting Notes
Degree of: Sweetness: ❶   Peatiness: ❹   Availability: ❹
Colour Light to mid-amber with gold highlights and just a tinge of green
Nose Quite fresh, light oak, quite light weight and dry; a little spirity
Flavour Dry with oaky tannins, of medium weight and lightly smoky
Finish Dry, oaky and chewy with dry tannins
Notes Gordon and MacPhail bottling

ST. MAGDALENE DISTILLER

Scapa **H**

Distillery	Scapa
Established	1885
Address	Kirkwall, Orkney
Map Ref.	HY 434089
Distillery No.	2

40% VOL — *Product of Scotland* — **70cl**

SCAPA
SINGLE HIGHLAND MALT SCOTCH WHISKY
Distilled **1983** *Distilled*
Trademark of Proprietors
TAYLOR & FERGUSON LTD · SCAPA · ORKNEY
SPECIALLY SELECTED, PRODUCED, MATURED & BOTTLED BY
AND UNDER THE RESPONSIBILITY OF
Gordon & Macphail
ELGIN · SCOTLAND · REGD. BOTTLER

History	Built by Macfarlane & Townsend. Owned by Hiram Walker (Now part of Allied Lyons) since 1954. The wash still was replaced by a "Lomond" still in 1959, this producing a heavier spirit than longer necked stills. Operated by Caledonian Malt Whisky Distillers.
Geography	Sited on the Lingro Burn two miles south west of Kirkwall on the A964 at the head of Scapa Bay.
Notes	For a malt with such a pronounced astringent nose, the palate is surprisingly sweet. Scapa Flow was where the German Fleet was scuttled at the end of World War 1. One of the main malts associated with Ballantine's blended Scotch Whisky.
Water	The Lingro Burn and nearby springs.

Age/Strength	*8 YEARS 57% abv*
Tasting Notes	
Degree of:	Sweetness: **8** Peatiness: **7** Availability: **4**
Colour	Peaty/amber with good gold highlights and a greenish tinge
Nose	Spirity, somewhat astringent, peaty
Flavour	Sweet, rich, full, lightly oaky, malty
Finish	Good, spicy and long-lasting
Notes	Gordon & MacPhail bottling

Age/Strength	*1965 DISTILLATION 24 YEARS 50.1% abv*
Tasting Notes	
Degree of:	Sweetness: **8** Peatiness: **6** Availability: **4**
Colour	Straw with lemony gold highlights
Nose	Sweet, quite fresh, rich and creamy peatiness with an underpinning of oak
Flavour	Quite sweet, smooth, softly peated, light and quite delicate
Finish	Smooth and smoky with a lanolin character
Notes	Wm. Cadenhead bottling - September 1990

The Singleton
of Auchroisk

Distillery	Auchroisk
Established	1974
Address	Mulben, Banffshire
Map Ref.	NJ 350512
Distillery No.	28
History	Managed by IDV which is part of Grand Metropolitan. Eight stills.
Geography	On the north side of the A95 between Keith and Aberlour.
Notes	A new distillery producing its first make in 1975. Despite being new, the buildings are well designed and blend in well with the surroundings. Sherry casks are used predominantly. Auchroisk is a showpiece distillery and has an old steam engine from Strathmill preserved in its entrance hall.
Water	Dorie's Well.

Age/Strength	*1976 DISTILLATION 40% abv*
Tasting Notes	
Degree of:	Sweetness: ❼ Peatiness: ❹ Availability: ❿
Colour	Amber with gold highlights
Nose	Rich, quite full and minty with a peach sweetness and good weight
Flavour	Quite full-bodied and smooth with a sherried nuttiness, a vanilla oaky oiliness and quite delicately peated
Finish	Quite long, nutty and dark with a smokiness on the tail
Notes	IDV bottling. Current vintage is 1981

Age/Strength	*1978 DISTILLATION 12 YEARS 59.3% abv*
Tasting Notes	
Degree of:	Sweetness: ❽ Peatiness: ❸ Availability: ❹
Colour	Pale straw with lemon/yellow highlights
Nose	Fresh, fruity - citrus and cherries, quite full with a touch of raisins at the back
Flavour	Sweet, fruity, smooth, round, good, oaky tannins and quite spirity
Finish	Smooth, spirity with a hint of cloves and quite long
Notes	Wm. Cadenhead bottling

Speyburn

Distillery	Speyburn
Established	1897
Address	Rothes, Moray
Map Ref.	NJ 273503
Distillery No.	38

History Built by the Speyburn-Glenlivet Distillery Company Ltd. Became part of DCL in 1916. Transferred to SMD in 1962. It was the first malt distillery to install a drum maltings, which closed in 1968. The distillery has two stills and is now owned by Inver House Distillers.

Geography Situated a quarter of a mile north west of the B9015 on the northern outskirts of Rothes.

Notes Speyburn started up in the last week of December in 1897. Doors and windows still had not been fitted to the stillhouse and, as a severe snowstorm was sweeping the district, employees had to work in overcoats. Just one butt of spirit was bonded with 1897 on its head.

Water The Granty (or Birchfield) Burn.

Age/Strength *10 YEARS 40% abv*

Tasting Notes

Degree of: Sweetness: ❽ Peatiness: ❷ Availability: ❻

Colour Very pale straw with lemon highlights

Nose Fresh, clean and aromatic with a rich, lemony fruitiness, medium-bodied and quite lightly peated

Flavour Fresh, clean, rich and medium-sweet; quite full-bodied

Finish Long and sweet with a touch of spice

Notes Inver House bottling

Age/Strength *1971 DISTILLATION 40% abv*

Tasting Notes

Degree of: Sweetness: ❽ Peatiness: ❺ Availability: ❹

Colour Rich, peaty/amber with good gold highlights

Nose Sweet, fruity, slightly spirity

Flavour Medium-sweet, lightish, smooth

Finish Mellow, reasonable length with oak on the end

Notes Gordon & MacPhail bottling

Springbank

Distillery	Springbank
Established	1828
Address	Campbeltown, Argyll
Map Ref.	NR 718205
Distillery No.	112

History Said to have been originally licensed to the Reid family. It was acquired by John and William Mitchell in 1837 and passed through various family hands until 1897 when the present owning company, J. & A. Mitchell & Company, was incorporated. Three stills.

Geography The distillery is in the centre of the town.

Notes The Campbeltown area once boasted around 30 distilleries. Springbank is now one of only two survivors. One of only three single malts still to be bottled at the distillery itself.

Water Crosshill Loch.

Age/Strength *10 YEARS 46% abv*

Tasting Notes

Degree of: Sweetness: **8** Peatiness: **5** Availability: **8**

Colour Pale straw, yellow highlights

Nose Lightish, sweetish, slight hints of coconut oil

Flavour Sweet, smooth, creamy, slight hint of coconut

Finish Good, smooth and distinctive

Age/Strength *15 YEARS 56% abv*

Tasting Notes

Degree of: Sweetness: **7** Peatiness: **5** Availability: **7**

Colour Light mid amber (honey coloured) with lemony highlights

Nose Medium weight, rich oily oak with a touch of greenness, quite lightly peated

Flavour Clean, smooth, medium-dry with good creamy oak and a touch of sweetness and greenness

Finish Long and smooth with a touch of tannin and hints of richness and saltiness on the tail

Springbank

Age/Strength	21 YEARS 46% abv
Tasting Notes	
Degree of:	Sweetness: **8** Peatiness: **5** Availability: **6**
Colour	Deep amber
Nose	Definite fruity notes, stickily sweet in their richness, also floral notes, a suggestion of coconut and medicinal cloves
Flavour	Silkily smooth, full bodied and creamy with a salty tang
Finish	Very fine, long, dark and oaky
Age/Strength	25 YEARS 46% abv
Tasting Notes	
Degree of:	Sweetness: **7** Peatiness: **6** Availability: **4**
Colour	Full, peaty amber with bronze highlights
Nose	Rich, ripe, sweet and full-bodied, smoky with a touch of ozone and oak
Flavour	Full, round, smoky and medium-sweet with oaky tannins and a salty tang
Finish	Long, smoky-oak and tangy with a touch of spiciness
Age/Strength	30 YEARS 46% abv
Tasting Notes	
Degree of:	Sweetness: **8** Peatiness: **6** Availability: **3**
Colour	Full amber with old gold highlights
Nose	Full and rich, almost raisiny with a touch of liquorice, almost tarry and medium-dry
Flavour	Sweet, rich, good fatty character, bitter chocolate and a salty tang
Finish	Long and tangy with good sweetness

SPRINGBANK DISTILLERY

143

Strathisla

Distillery	Strathisla
Established	1786
Address	Keith, Banffshire
Map Ref.	NJ 429511
Distillery No.	32

History Built as Milltown (Keith was the centre of the Scottish linen industry) and later known as Milton, Strathisla was originally the name of the make and subsequently became that of the distillery also. The distillery was twice badl[y] damaged in the 1870s, first by fire in 1876 and three years late[r] as the result of an explosion. Extensive modernisation took pla[ce] after these events and again in 1965, when the distillery was enlarged from two to six stills. It is today owned by Chivas Brothers Ltd, a subsidiary of The Seagram Company of Cana[da]

Geography Half a mile from the centre of Keith.

Notes The reservoir where the water supply is collected is said to be visited nightly by "the water kelpies" which could account for [a] special flavour.

Water The Broomhill Spring.

Age/Strength *8 YEARS 40% abv*

Tasting Notes

Degree of: Sweetness: ❽ Peatiness: ❸ Availability: ❹

Colour Amber with good gold highlights

Nose Fruity, spirity, sweet lanolin oiliness

Flavour Spicy, medium-sweet, touch of oak, quite smooth

Finish Good body, perhaps a little short

Notes Gordon & MacPhail bottling

Age/Strength *12 YEARS 40% abv*

Tasting Notes

Degree of: Sweetness: ❽ Peatiness: ❸ Availability: ❹

Colour Bright gold/straw

Nose Full, sweet, fruity, appley, very pronounced and rich

Flavour Rich, warm, quite full, sweet

Finish Long, fine and mellow

Strathisla

Age/Strength	*21 YEARS 40% abv*
Tasting Notes	
Degree of:	Sweetness: ❽ Peatiness: ❹ Availability: ❹
Colour	Amber with bright copper highlights
Nose	Medium-sweet, malty, lightly peated and oaky
Flavour	Medium-dry, oaky, spicy and creamy
Finish	Long and spicy with hints of bitter chocolate
Notes	Gordon and MacPhail bottling

Strathmill

Distillery	Strathmill
Established	1891
Address	Keith, Banffshire
Map Ref.	NJ 425502
Distillery No.	33
History	Originally a corn and flour mill, it was converted in 1891 as Glenisla-Glenlivet. Acquired by W. & A. Gilbey in 1895, when it was renamed Strathmill. Became part of IDV in 1962 and now absorbed into Grand Metropolitan. Doubled from two to four stills in late 1960s.
Geography	Sited within 100 yards of the turning on to the B9014 from Keith to Dufftown.
Notes	Very rarely available as a single, the make largely goes into the J. & B. blend. The above label has not been used for thirty years.
Water	A spring at the distillery.
Age/Strength	*12 YEARS 55.5% abv*
Tasting Notes	
Degree of:	Sweetness: ❻ Peatiness: ❸ Availability: ❶
Colour	Very pale watery with watery green highlights
Nose	Light, cerealy, lightly smoky with a touch of perfume and a delicate nuttiness
Flavour	Medium-sweet, smooth and quite round with good body
Finish	Long and spicy with a pleasant leafy greenness
Notes	Cask sample from J. & B. Scotland Ltd who kindly supplied the above label from their archives. The whisky is not now available

Talisker

Distillery	Talisker
Established	1831
Address	Carbost, Isle of Skye
Map Ref.	NG 377318
Distillery No.	63

ISLE OF SKYE
TALISKER
SINGLE MALT SCOTCH WHISKY

Beyond Carbost Village close to the Shore is a gentle haven sheltered from the bleak ravines which sweep down to the coast. Here in the shadow of the distant Cuillin Hills lies the island's only distillery Talisker. The Golden Spirit of Skye has more than a hint of local seaweed peppered with sour & sweet notes and a memorable warm peaty finish.

45.8% VOL TALISKER DISTILLERY CARBOST SKYE 70 cl €

History — The distillery was originally sited at Snizort, to the north of the island, but closed and mysteriously moved. Founded by Hugh and Kenneth MacAskill. Rebuilt 1880-87 and extended in 1900. Merged into Dailuaine-Talisker Distilleries in 1898, under which name it still trades although absorbed fully into the DCL in 1925. Operated by SMD. Rebuilt in 1960 after a stillhouse fire. Five stills.

Geography — Situated in a gentle bowl which forms a lonely, very sheltered glen on the west coast of Skye.

Notes — The only distillery on the island of Skye, it took its name from farm about six miles distant. The make was triple distilled until 1928. One of United Distillers' *Classic Malts.*

Water — From the Carbost Burn on the slopes of Cnoc Nan Speireag (Stockveil Hill).

Age/Strength — *10 YEARS 45.8% abv*
Tasting Notes
Degree of: Sweetness: ❶ Peatiness: ❿ Availability: ❿
Colour Straw with gold highlights
Nose Pungent, peaty, burnt heather, hints of ozone
Flavour Peaty, dry, spicy, quite creamy
Finish Smoky, spicy, smooth, almost salty at the end

Age/Strength — *8 YEARS 45.8% abv*
Tasting Notes
Degree of: Sweetness: ❶ Peatiness: ❿ Availability: ❿
Colour Lovely amber with green highlights
Nose Pungent, full and peaty, but soft
Flavour Dry, spicy, full, with a lot of smokiness
Finish Long with a burst of flavour on swallowing

Tamdhu S

Distillery	Tamdhu
Established	1897
Address	Knockando, Moray
Map Ref.	NJ 189418
Distillery No.	44

History Built by the Tamdhu Distillery Company Ltd. which was owned by a consortium of blenders. Owned by Highland Distilleries Company since 1898. Closed from 1927-47 but extended in 1972 from two to four stills and again to six stills in 1975. A feature is its Saladin Maltings, largely rebuilt.

Geography Sited on the banks of the River Spey south of the B9102 between Knockando and Archiestown.

Notes The old railway station at Knockando has been converted into a visitor centre for Tamdhu. Tamdhu does not have the traditional pagoda heads atop its kilns, having instead a short, square concrete chimney. The only distillery to malt all its own barley on site.

Water A spring under the distillery.

Age/Strength *10 YEARS 40% abv*
Tasting Notes
Degree of: Sweetness: **8**   Peatiness: **4**   Availability: **9**
Colour Pale golden, amber highlights
Nose Lightish with a hint of sweetness akin to apples
Flavour Round, mellow, sweet and slightly spicy and peaty
Finish Soft, creamily smooth and smoky

Age/Strength *NO AGE STATEMENT 40% abv*
Tasting Notes
Degree of: Sweetness: **7**   Peatiness: **4**   Availability: **9**
Colour Straw/amber with yellow highlights
Nose Medium-bodied, fruity and a touch floral, medium-sweet with a greenness
Flavour Medium-sweet, quite light, mashy, biscuity and quite smooth
Finish Quite short, spirity and sweet

Tamnavulin

TAMNAVULIN
Glenlivet
S I N G L E
M A L T
S C O T C H
W H I S K Y
DISTILLED, MATURED & BOTTLED IN SCOTLAND
TAMNAVULIN-GLENLIVET DISTILLERY CO. LTD.,
TOMNAVOULIN, SCOTLAND

40% vol   70 cl

Distillery	Tamnavulin
Established	1966
Address	Tomnavoulin, Banffshire
Map Ref.	NJ 213260
Distillery No.	67

History | Built by the Tamnavulin-Glenlivet Distillery Company, a subsidiary of Invergordon Distillers. A very modern distillery, it can be operated by just a handful of technicians.

Geography Notes | Sited on the east side of the B9008 at the village of Tomnavouli. The only distillery actually positioned on the river Livet, from which the cooling and other process waters are drawn. Tomnavoulin in Gaelic means "mill on the hill" and an old carding mill which stands on the river just below the distillery has been converted into a very attractive visitor centre. The mi. machinery has been preserved inside. Equally pleasant are the grassy banks of the river which have been turned into a picnic area. Tamnavulin is naturally light in colour, taking any colour has from the casks in which it is matured, no caramel being added to the make.

Water | Subterranean springs at Easterton in the local hills.

Age/Strength | *10 YEARS 40% abv*
Tasting Notes
Degree of: | Sweetness: **9**   Peatiness: **3**   Availability: **8**
Colour | Very pale straw with golden highlights
Nose | Light, sweet with a slightly floral edge
Flavour | Mature, sweet, light, gently oaky
Finish | Long, easy and slightly spicy

Age/Strength | *18 YEARS 46% abv*
Tasting Notes
Degree of: | Sweetness: **8**   Peatiness: **3**   Availability: **4**
Colour | Very dark, teak coloured
Nose | Nutty, quite spirity, light and medium-sweet
Flavour | Smooth, oaky, quite velvety and nutty
Finish | Smooth, spirity, quite long with a dry end
Notes | Wm. Cadenhead bottling

Teaninich H

Distillery	Teaninich
Established	1817
Address	Alness, Ross-shire
Map Ref.	NH 653691

> HIGHLAND
> SINGLE MALT
> SCOTCH WHISKY
>
> The Cromarty Firth is one of the few places in the British Isles inhabited by PORPOISE. They can be seen quite regularly, swimming close to the shore less than a mile from
>
> ## TEANINICH
>
> distillery founded in 1817 in the Ross-shire town of ALNESS, the distillery is now one of the largest in Scotland. TEANINICH is an assertive single MALT WHISKY with a spicy, smoky, satisfying taste.
>
> A G E D 10 Y E A R S
> 43% vol   70 cl

History	Founded by Captain Hugo Munro. An entirely new distillation unit named "A side" began production in 1970. "B side", the milling, mashing and fermentation part of the old distillery was rebuilt in 1973. Ten stills. Now owned by United Distillers plc.
Geography	Sited to the south of the A9 on the western outskirts of Alness and on the west bank of the River Alness, three quarters of a mile from its outlet into the Cromarty Firth.
Notes	Barnard recorded in 1887 that Teaninich was the only distillery north of Inverness to be "Lighted by electricity". In 1925 both malting floors were of solid clay. Closed.
Water	Dairywell Spring.

Age/Strength	*10 YEARS 43% abv*
Tasting Notes	
Degree of:	Sweetness: ❼ Peatiness: ❺ Availability: ❻
Colour	Pale straw with yellow highlights and a tinge of lemon
Nose	Fresh, quite light with a good green peatiness, medium-sweet with an appley character
Flavour	Medium-dry, gently smoky, smooth and round
Finish	Clean and fresh with a sweet tail
Notes	United Distillers bottling

Age/Strength	*17 YEARS 43% abv*
Tasting Notes	
Degree of:	Sweetness: ❾ Peatiness: ❸ Availability: ❷
Colour	Quite pale straw with lemon highlights
Nose	Quite full, spirity and fresh, almost salty, fruity and floral
Flavour	Quite sweet, round, spicy, full-bodied, rich and delicately peated with a nutty character
Finish	Long, sweet and slightly smoky
Notes	Master of Malt bottling cask no. 13984

Distillery	Tobermory
Established	1798
Address	Tobermory, Isle of Mull
Map Ref.	NM 504551
Distillery No.	81

LEDAIG
SINGLE MALT
FROM
THE ISLE OF MULL.

1974
Vintage

BOTTLED 1992

This rare old single malt whisky
was distilled at the Ledaig Distillery
on the Isle of Mull by
Ledaig Distillers (Tobermory) Ltd.

PRODUCE OF SCOTLAND

70cl   43%Vol

History — Established by one John Sinclair. Taken over by DCL in 1916. Silent 1930-72. Now owned by a Yorkshire-based property company. Four stills.

Geography — Sited at the head of Tobermory Bay.

Notes — The only distillery on Mull. The distillery was also known as "Ledaig" until 1978 when it was renamed Tobermory. It has also been referred to as "Mull". Bottlings of the malt can be found under the name of Ledaig, while Tobermory is presently a vatted malt.

Water — Misnish Lochs.

Age/Strength — *TOBERMORY NO AGE STATEMENT 40% abv*
Tasting Notes
Degree of: — Sweetness: ❷   Peatiness: ❽   Availability: ❸
Colour — Pale golden
Nose — Fruity, fairly light
Flavour — Soft, well balanced, smooth, slightly sweet edge
Finish — Finishes smokily and rather woody

Age/Strength — *LEDAIG 1974 DISTILLATION 18 YEARS 43% abv*
Tasting Notes
Degree of: — Sweetness: ❷   Peatiness: ❾   Availability: ❺
Colour — Medium-pale, lemony-gold
Nose — Medium-bodied, woody almost with a slight greenness and smokiness at the back and an almost Christmas cake yeasty character
Flavour — Medium-bodied, oaky with a slight greenness and good richness at the back
Finish — Good length with a green smoky tail

Tomatin

Distillery	Tomatin
Established	1897
Address	Tomatin, Inverness-shire
Map Ref.	NH 790295
Distillery No.	64

TOMATIN
SINGLE *Highland* MALT
SCOTCH WHISKY
AGED 10 YEARS
DISTILLED AND BOTTLED IN SCOTLAND BY THE TOMATIN DISTILLERY CO LTD

History | Founded by the Tomatin Spey District Distillery Company Ltd. Extended from two to four stills in 1956, to six in 1958, to ten in 1961, to eleven in 1964 and finally to twenty three in 1974.

Geography | Sited on the west of the A9 at the village of Tomatin, 12 miles south of Inverness. At 1,028 feet above sea level it is one of Scotland's highest distilleries.

Notes | The first distillery to be owned by a Japanese company and with the potential for the highest output (more than 12 million litres of alcohol) of all the malt distilleries. In Gaelic Tomatin means "the hill of bushes". Bottled by Tomatin Distillery Company.

Water | Alt-Na-Frithe (a local burn).

Age/Strength | *10 YEARS 43% abv*
Tasting Notes
Degree of: | Sweetness: ❻ Peatiness: ❺ Availability: ❺
Colour | Straw with yellowy gold highlights
Nose | Dryish, malty, leafy, spirity with a sweet edge
Flavour | Medium-sweet, smooth, soft, round, slightly smoky
Finish | Spicy, lightly peaty, slightly grapey

Age/Strength | *1976 DISTILLATION 13 YEARS 60.5% abv*
Tasting Notes
Degree of: | Sweetness: ❻ Peatiness: ❺ Availability: ❹
Colour | Pale amber with gold highlights
Nose | Medium weight, a touch of green hedgerows, fresh with light oak, medium sweet with a light smokiness at the back
Flavour | Medium-sweet, clean, tangy and lightly smoky
Finish | Quite sweet and spicy with good length
Notes | Wm. Cadenhead bottling

Age/Strength	*1966 DISTILLATION 26 YEARS 43% abv*
Tasting Notes	
Degree of:	Sweetness: **❺** Peatiness: **❹** Availability: **❷**
Colour	Very pale straw with a tinge of green
Nose	Clean, fresh, medium-sweet, spirity, cerealy, touch of perfume
Flavour	Medium-dry, light and smooth with a touch of appley fruit
Finish	Quite clean, medium length with a touch of greenness
Notes	Master of Malt bottling cask no. 1432-65

Tomintoul

S

Distillery	Tomintoul
Established	1964
Address	nr. Tomintoul, Banffshire
Map Ref.	NJ 149254
Distillery No.	59
History	A modern distillery, production only began in 1965 and it was not until 1972 that the make began to appear in bottle. Built by the Tomintoul Distillery Ltd and bought by Scottish & Universal Investment Trust (part of Lonhro) in 1973. Managed by Whyte & Mackay which was bought from Lonhro by Brent Walker towards the end of 1988. Doubled from two to four stills in 1974.
Geography	Situated in the valley of the River Avon on the A939 Grantown-on-Spey to Bridge of Avon road.
Notes	Tomintoul is the highest village in the Scottish Highlands although the distillery itself is not quite as high above sea level as Dalwhinnie. Tomintoul is regularly cut off by snow in winter.
Water	The Ballantruan Spring.

Age/Strength	*8 YEARS 40% abv*
Tasting Notes	
Degree of:	Sweetness: **❼** Peatiness: **❼** Availability: **❶**
Colour	Gold with yellow highlights
Nose	Light with a hint of sweetness and richness
Flavour	Lightish, sweet, clean and creamy
Finish	Good with a light fragrant touch

Tomintoul

Age/Strength	*12 YEARS 40% abv*
Tasting Notes	
Degree of:	Sweetness: **7** Peatiness: **3** Availability: **8**
Colour	Peaty straw with good gold highlights
Nose	Medium-sweet, rich, spirity, vanilla, fruity - almost orangey
Flavour	Medium-sweet, lightish, slightly peppery, oaky
Finish	Spirity, spicy, quite smooth, the oaky flavour lingers

Tormore S

Distillery	Tormore
Established	1958
Address	Advie, Grantown-on-Spey, Moray
Map Ref.	NJ 154350
Distillery No.	61
History	Built 1958-60 by Long John Distillers Ltd. Now part of Allied Lyons and operated by Caledonian Malt Distillers. Doubled from four to eight stills in 1972.
Geography	South of the A95 between Grantown-on-Spey and the Bridge of Avon.
Notes	The first new Highland malt distillery to be built in the 20th century. The distillery and associated housing are of most striking design, the work of Sir Arthur Richardson, a past president of the Royal Academy.
Water	The Achvochkie Burn.

Age/Strength	*10 YEARS 40% abv*
Tasting Notes	
Degree of:	Sweetness: **8** Peatiness: **3** Availability: **8**
Colour	Pale golden
Nose	Light, delicate, sometimes described as flinty; unusual dryness
Flavour	Slightly sweet, of medium weight and slightly spirity
Finish	Fine, distinguished and long

Tullibardine

PRODUCT OF SCOTLAND

Tullibardine

SINGLE HIGHLAND MALT SCOTCH WHISKY

A Single Malt Scotch Whisky of quality and distinction distilled and bottled by

TULLIBARDINE DISTILLERY LIMITED
BLACKFORD   PERTHSHIRE   SCOTLAND

40% vol   70cl

Distillery	Tullibardine
Established	1949
Address	Blackford, Perthshire
Map Ref.	NN 896087
Distillery No.	85
History	There was a previous Tullibardine distillery near Blackford which was established in 1798, although its exact location is not known. The new distillery was the work of Delme Evans, who also established Jura and Glenallachie. Owned by Invergordon Distillers since 1971. Rebuilt in 1973-74 and enlarged from two to four stills.
Geography	Situated south of the A9 on the south western outskirts of the village of Blackford, four miles south of Auchterarder.
Notes	On the site of an ancient brewery, the distillery takes its name from the nearby Tullibardine Moor, home of Gleneagles Hotel and golf courses. This area has always been famed for its water e.g. Highland Spring is from Blackford. Tradition has it that the fair Queen Helen of Scotland was drowned at a ford on the Allan River, hence the name Blackford.
Water	The Danny Burn.
Age/Strength	*10 YEARS 40% abv*
Tasting Notes	
Degree of:	Sweetness: ❸ Peatiness: ❻ Availability: ❻
Colour	Straw, goldy-green highlights
Nose	Quite full, soft, malty and earthy
Flavour	Dryish, spicy, with a richness and roundness, quite smooth
Finish	Peppery, warm and quite long, slightly bitter at the end

Vatted Malts

ge/Strength
sting Notes

GLENCOE 12 YEARS 40% abv

Degree of: Sweetness: **8**   Peatiness: **4**   Availability: **4**
Colour Bright, mid-amber with lemony gold highlights
Nose Malty, spirity with an apple character, quite full-bodied, medium-dry with a touch of peat
Flavour Medium-dry, round and smooth, appley with good body
Finish Quite sweet and of good length

ge/Strength
sting Notes

OLD ELGIN 8 YEARS 40% abv

Degree of: Sweetness: **7**   Peatiness: **6**   Availability: **4**
Colour Mid amber with gold highlights
Nose Medium-full-bodied, medium-dry and smoky with a touch of greenness and dark, appley fruit
Flavour Rich, medium-sweet, quite full-bodied and peppery; fresh, round and smooth
Finish Fresh, medium-sweet and clean
Notes Gordon and MacPhail bottling

ge/Strength
sting Notes

POIT DHUBH 12 YEARS

Degree of: Sweetness: **6**   Peatiness: **4**   Availability: **3**
Colour Amber with good yellow highlights
Nose Medium-sweet, slightly green fruit and quite rich
Flavour Smooth, a touch of dryness, lightly peated, quite elegant, although light
Finish Long, smoky and slightly perfumed

ge/Strength
sting Notes

PRIDE OF ISLAY 10 YEARS 40% abv

Degree of: Sweetness: **1**   Peatiness: **10**   Availability: **4**
Colour Mid amber with yellowy gold highlights
Nose Full-bodied and smoky with rich, chocolatey nuttiness
Flavour Big, smoky, quite pungent and bone dry with a slight edge of richness
Finish Full, long and smoky with a slight tang of bitter chocolate
Notes Gordon and MacPhail bottling

Vatted Malts (Cont.)

Age/Strength	*PRIDE OF THE LOWLANDS 12 YEARS 40% abv*
Tasting Notes	
Degree of:	Sweetness: ❸ Peatiness: ❷ Availability: ❹
Colour	Amber with yellow gold highlights
Nose	Medium-weight, fresh, oily-rich and medium-dry with a slight unripe grapey character
Flavour	Smooth, medium-dry with a touch of coffee and good richness medium-weight
Finish	Quite long and fresh with the tang of coffee on the tail
Notes	Gordon and MacPhail bottling

Age/Strength	*PRIDE OF ORKNEY 12 YEARS 40% abv*
Tasting Notes	
Degree of:	Sweetness: ❷ Peatiness: ❺ Availability: ❹
Colour	Light to mid-amber with gold highlights
Nose	Quite light and rich, dried fruit characters with hints of honey
Flavour	Off-dry, smooth, lightly smoky and malty
Finish	Clean with a refreshing greenness
Notes	Gordon and MacPhail bottling

Age/Strength	*PRIDE OF STRATHSPEY 12 YEARS 40% abv*
Tasting Notes	
Degree of:	Sweetness: ❽ Peatiness: ❸ Availability: ❹
Colour	Amber with gold highlights
Nose	Medium-sweet, a touch of creamy oiliness, rich oak and a hint nuttiness
Flavour	Medium-sweet, quite full-bodied, smooth and round with a hazelnut character
Finish	Long and nutty with a dry edge and nice oaky tannins
Notes	Gordon and MacPhail bottling

Age/Strength	*SHEEP DIP 8 YEARS 40% abv*
Tasting Notes	
Degree of:	Sweetness: ❸ Peatiness: ❻ Availability: ❻
Colour	Pale amber with good yellow highlights
Nose	Dry, softly peated and slightly green
Flavour	Dry, but with nice richness, spicy, good peatiness, round and medium-bodied
Finish	Gentle smokiness and medium length

Vatted Malts

Age/Strength	*SPEYSIDE 8 YEARS*
Tasting Notes	
Degree of:	Sweetness: **8** Peatiness: **3** Availability: **3**
Colour	Straw with good yellowy green highlights
Nose	Fresh, spirity, mealy and malty
Flavour	Sweet, smooth, round and soft
Finish	Malty, spicy and quite long

Single Malts
from Independent Bottlers

Age/Strength	*ASKAIG 1978 DISTILLATION 15 YEARS* 43% *abv*
Tasting Notes	
Degree of:	Sweetness: **1** Peatiness: **9** Availability: **2**
Colour	Very pale straw, almost watery, with a green tinge
Nose	Medium-bodied, quite heavily peated, a slight ozone character with a burnt touch
Flavour	Dry, salty, fresh burnt character, smooth and round
Finish	Smoky, of reasonable length and smooth
Notes	Single Islay malt bottled by Master of Malt

Age/Strength	*FINLAGGAN 1979 DISTILLATION* 43% *abv*
Tasting Notes	
Degree of:	Sweetness: **1** Peatiness: **9** Availability: **3**
Colour	Very pale straw with lemony-yellow highlights
Nose	Full and pungent with an earthy smokiness with fresh hints of ozone
Flavour	Dry, smoky and fresh, clean and big-bodied
Finish	Long, smooth and rich with a smoky-burnt oakiness
Notes	The Vintage Malt Whisky Company bottling

Single Malts (Cont.)

Age/Strength	*MACPHAIL'S MALT 10 YEARS 40% abv*
Tasting Notes	
Degree of:	Sweetness: ❹ Peatiness: ❼ Availability: ❹
Colour	Mid amber with old gold highlights
Nose	Quite light, fresh, dark and smoky, medium-dry
Flavour	Medium-dry, good body, an earthy peatiness and a touch of spiciness
Finish	Fresh, quite smoky and long lasting with a touch of oak
Notes	Single malt bottling under Gordon and MacPhail's own label

Age/Strength	*OAK BRANDY CASK 1963 40% abv*
Tasting Notes	
Degree of:	Sweetness: ❻ Peatiness: ❸ Availability: ❶
Colour	Pale amber with yellow gold highlights
Nose	Quite light weight, medium-dry with a green fruity character,
Flavour	Spirity with a hint of acetone and malty
Finish	Quite long, dark, cough linctus character and lightly smoky
Notes	A single Speyside malt matured in a brandy cask and bottled by Gordon and MacPhail

Age/Strength	*OAK BRANDY CASK 1963 40% abv*
Tasting Notes	
Degree of:	Sweetness: ❺ Peatiness: ❸ Availability: ❶
Colour	Amber with gold highlights
Nose	Medium-sweet and medium-bodied with a hint of smokiness and a rich, honeyed character
Flavour	Medium-dry, soft, quite light and fresh with a touch of richness
Finish	Quite long with a dry finish and a touch of honey on the tail
Notes	A single Speyside malt matured in a brandy cask and bottled by Gordon and MacPhail in 1983

Age/Strength	*OAK PORT CASK 1967 40% abv*
Tasting Notes	
Degree of:	Sweetness: ❺ Peatiness: ❺ Availability: ❶
Colour	Amber with gold highlights
Nose	Medium-sweet, quite rich, with a ripe Christmas cake fruitiness and a slight touch of perfume on the tail
Flavour	Medium-dry, quite round with demerara sugar character lightly smoky, dark and nutty
Finish	Long, quite dry and chewy
Notes	A single Speyside malt matured in a port cask and bottled by Gordon and MacPhail in 1993

Single Malts (Cont.)

Age/Strength	*SELECT CASK 12 YEARS 43% abv*
Tasting Notes	
Degree of:	Sweetness: ❽ Peatiness: ❸ Availability: ❷
Colour	Medium pale, old gold with a quite rich centre
Nose	Full-bodied, good richness, lightly peated with an oily nuttiness, ripe almonds and almost banana fruit
Flavour	Medium-sweet, a touch of spice, quite full and round
Finish	Long, quite rich and smoky with a touch of oaky vanilla
Notes	Master of Malt Select Cask bottling from cask nos. 10632/38

Age/Strength	*TANTALLON 13 YEARS 43% abv*
Tasting Notes	
Degree of:	Sweetness: ❽ Peatiness: ❹ Availability: ❷
Colour	Amber with good gold highlights
Nose	Medium-bodied, rich, sweet, toffee-like, lightly peated with an appley flavour
Flavour	Sweet, rich, quite full, round, and smooth and slightly oily
Finish	Long and sweet with a toffee character and a chewy tail
Notes	Single malt bottled for The Vintage Whisky Company

ACKNOWLEDGEMENTS

Our grateful thanks are due to a great many people for their assistance in completing this edition: From the distilling companies, in alphabetical order: Joan Mackie of Caledonian Malt Whisky Distillers; Alex Ross at Ben Nevis; Ian MacMillan, Fergus Hartley and Robin Dods from Burn Stewart; Sheelagh Croskery at Bushmills; Ross Gunn of Glenlivet; Peter Fairlie at Glenturret; Simon Trevor and Aleta Donaldson of Matthew Gloag; David Stewart of William Grant; John Grant, Malcolm Greenwood of Glenfarclas; John Way and Iain Kennedy of IDV; Julian Rowett, Jacqui Campbell and Bob Homewood of Invergordon; Alistair Douglas and Jacqui Stacey of Inver House; Tom Smith of J. & B. Scotland; Jim Turle of Lang Brothers; Andrew MacDonald of Macallan-Glenlivet; Amanda Templeman of Macdonald and Muir; George Hocknull and Jim McColl of Morrison Bowmore; John Ashworth of J.R. Phillips; Gordon Wright at Springbank; Stephen Nettleton of Tobermory Distillers; Richard Paterson and Margaret Nicol of Whyte & Mackay; Andy Tinlin of United Distillers. From the independent bottlers: David and Ian Urquhart and Sarah Watson of Gordon and MacPhail; Neil Clapperton of Cadenhead's; Brian Crook of The Vintage Malt Whisky Company; Andrew and Brian Symington of Signatory; Christie's for the use of photograph on page 120. And Mike Fluskey.

Our sincere apologies to anyone who has been omitted from the above list, but when an endeavour such as this takes some time to complete, as this has done, memory deteriorates with age. You know who you are - we thank you.

The Malt Whisky Association was formed to promote the appreciation and enjoyment of single malt whisky. It offers members an exclusive selection of whiskies by mail order, including both single malts and rare, hard to track down bottlings. Some of these *Master of Malt* whiskies are available only to members. Regular special offers give members big savings on many of these whiskies.

Our Membership Information Pack includes latest offers and malt whisky information, a list of opening times for those distilleries that welcome visitors and details of top value miniature selections. To obtain a pack send £1 in stamps or coins to cover post and packing (overseas £2 or U.S. $3 or equivalent) to:

Vann Ross, Membership Secretary, The Malt Whisky Association, Largs, Ayrshire, Scotland KA30 8BR.

Also available from the above address is The Malt Whisky Map of Scotland. To obtain a copy, send £4 cheque or cash. (£5 overseas. Payment by cash, Eurocard, Mastercard or Visa only, please).

ABOUT THE AUTHORS

John Lamond

A past president of The Institute of Wines and Spirits (Scotland), John has worked in the Scottish licensed trade for most of his life. Born and brought up in Scotland, his knowledge of single malts is unsurpassed. In 1987, he came first in a national competition to find Britain's *Master of Malt*, no small achievement in a field of some 600 entrants. He is also the author of *The Whisky Connoisseur's Companion*, writes regularly about malt whisky and leads frequent malt whisky tastings, both in Scotland and overseas.

Robin Tucek

Founder of *The Malt Whisky Association*, Robin is a journalist whose particular interest is malt whisky. This led to the idea of forming a club for all malt whisky lovers and so the Association was born in 1988. He wanted to produce a definitive background and tasting reference work to help further the enjoyment of malt whisky. It was important, he felt, to guide rather than tell the reader which malts to like. Robin and John met through *The Master of Malt* competition, which he was promoting. The first edition of *The Malt File* soon followed.